Titles by *Langaa* RPCIG

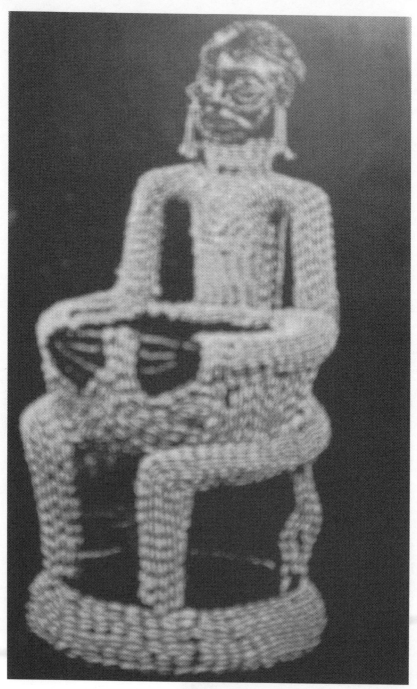

Ŋgòn Nso

A Basket
of Kola Nuts

Bongasu Tanla Kishani

Langaa Research & Publishing CIG
Mankon, Bamenda

Publisher:
Langaa RPCIG
(Langaa Research & Publishing Common Initiative Group)
P.O. Box 902 Mankon
Bamenda
North West Region
Cameroon
Langaagrp@gmail.com
www.langaapublisher.com

Distributed outside N. America by African Books Collective
orders@africanbookscollective.com
www.africanbookscollective.com

Distributed in N. America by Michigan State University Press
msupress@msu.edu
www.msupress.msu.edu

ISBN: 9956-558-55-9

DISCLAIMER

This is a work of fiction. Names, characters, places, and incidents are either the author's invention or they are used fictitiously. Any resemblance to actual places and persons, living or dead, events, or locales is coincidental.

Contents

Dedication

In Memory of My Father,
Moósér Kíshaàne Yeèkpu Kòŋnyùy
(1902 –1980)

And

To

My Mother,
Regina Tanlaka Lámé Taàlúkòŋ

Preface

A Basket of Kola Nuts has an unusual story to tell about its beginnings. Thieves broke into my house in Yawunde on November 26th 2006 and stole my IBM computer laptop, containing the first draft of the present text together with three manuscripts of books as well as some of my belongings. So, fortunately or unfortunately, the present text owes its own concrete life to the theft of that earlier draft, since it might not have seen the light of day in the same form, if the first version had survived in my possession. Consequently, instead of lying down, I had to confront the theft as a challenge by trying to write the current text almost anew. In fact, I have since had to rework this present version through earlier drafts and pertinent ideas I could lay my hands on here and there in my house, mind or elsewhere.

Although both texts are still somehow alike, I would have finished the first draft by early 2007. So, besides delaying my entire work, the theft of my laptop containing the drafts of my books did cost a lot of time. Today, *A Basket of Kola Nuts* is like *vox clamantis in desertis* (a voice calling out from the wilderness), specifically against stealing. And even if, like evil in general, it has never been eradicated from human society, theft is still an undesirable element in human life. Thieves ever practice it at their own risks. As a Cameroonian, I was quite surprised to find from all evidences that an Assistant-commander of a *Gendarmerie Brigarde* then at Nkomo was in possession of my City phone, which the thieves had made away with after breaking into my house. His conversation with the Police revealed that he was somehow sheltering the thieves and was in turn not only being sheltered by some of his colleagues who tried to lobby me into an *arrangement* with him, instead of bringing him to face justice, but also has still been moving around scot-free. The only practical way of bringing him before the law is to buy back my possessions as well as the money the thieves stole from my house. So, I chose to use remnants of my money to live and wonder about the whole issue. But, is it because the truth at times hides as if in a lie, when one *steals* a glance at someone in the mirror or when one *steals* a march on someone else; or is it because justice as part and parcel of human life never punishes every theft that some traditions allow one to still *steal* a certain permissible quantity of kola nuts during a kola harvest or as the Nso' say 'God can *steal* a child' and one can also *steal* the Fon's hands to thank someone else, that such burglaries still continue unchecked in Cameroon or elsewhere?

Far from it! A Christian or an evangelical conception of stealing is at once pedagogical, subtle and wise. It presents two thieves with Christ on the cross, and calls for vigilance and a choice to act like one of them. Though one may never know exactly when a thief comes to steal, Christ presents but the value of what it means for a thief to repent or not to do so. The one merits forgiveness at the crucial moment of redemption just as it was the case of the repentant thief with whom Christ was crucified and to whom he chose to promise paradise as a reward for his repentance. So, as Christians we all admire both the repentance and the promise. Repentance is an aspect of a change of mentality about which Christianity has been preaching and wrestling for ages since John the Baptist who came before Jesus Christ, presented himself, as *vox clamantis in desertis* (Lk. 3, 4).

In a way, therefore, *A Basket of Kola Nuts* is a kind of *Vox Clamantis In Desertis* by dint of the story of its composition, themes and plea for a change of some of our attitudes and mentalities towards the kola plant and its fruits or certain erroneous moral values on the one hand, and towards certain perceptions of the interface of content and form in the poetic genre on the other hand. For, by taking the form of its literate, oraural and sculptural containers, poetic genre differs as its contents and forms interact as if in respect of the scholastic adage whereby every container shapes its contents according to its form. *A Basket of Kola Nuts* tries to show not only that life, far from being an opposition between, is rather an interface of, content and form, politics and religion, scientific and non-scientific disciplines, metaphysics and physics, etc, but also that it draws the reader's attention towards exploring plural theories as concrete experiences rather than otherwise.

So technically, poetry like every other discipline needs to be revamped not only as holistic and dynamic, but also as interdisciplinary and concrete in its content and forms. Plaiting baskets of poetic kola nuts offered me an opportunity to aspire towards this goal, especially as each idea therein serves as a rope one stretches in its literate and oraural length of artistic shapes and contents. The shape of each basket internally spells the form in terms of metre and rhythm. Contents follow the shape of the container in like manner that the container gives the shape or form of the contents. Varieties of kola baskets contain kola messages as kola lobes, kola pods and kola nuts for each and every reader first to pick and choose, and then to chew and discuss as in a dialogue or conversation with the author. Besides offering readably edible therapeutic kola, our apparently sole poetic text intends to present to speakers and listeners, or writers and readers, a text in which composition and comprehension though surviving somehow within a specific cultural framework, nevertheless invites and brings both audience and authors together in the world of live dialogues or conversations. *A Basket of Kola Nuts* like the kola lobe or kola nut, we share and eat together initiates conversations and dialogues of various kinds the world over.

The text of *A Basket of Kola Nuts* therefore aims at an interdisciplinary approach to the comprehension of reality. Every artistic, literate and oraural perspective of each discipline such as anthropology, art, biology, chemistry, economics, geology, linguistics, literature, mathematics, physics, philosophy, poetry, religion, science of education, sociology, etc, is called upon to walk as arm in arm as it works hand in hand with one another whether they live a hand to-mouth-existence or in opulence. Whatever is the case, no discipline survives alone. In itself, our text therefore, neither exclusively addresses solely poetry nor any of the disciplines, taken in isolation. The ideal of nobody is an island finds one of its concrete expressions here, as no discipline is an island. Its main aim is to depict a certain way of life, entertain our readers and rationally appeal to or titillate everybody. Such an aim obliged our efforts in this poetic art to take a particular slant that sets philosophical issues into interplay, in order to draw attention to every species of kola as a commodity of common usage and discourse that always animates intellectual and social life: '*He / She who brings kola brings life*'. Its realism exercises our imagination to dream about the concrete facts of life rather than merely about theories that may never separate one from a sheer Cartesian itch.

Both craftsmanship and crafts-woman-ship call for a renewal with common sense as well as in the ethical or moral common places of wondering and speculation that isolate and stress at the same time the primacy of such key issues as poetic imagination with the naked decency and horrendous surprise of scorn, truth and violence. For, as a portrait of art in the arts, *A Basket of Kola Nuts* is a concrete long poem we weave in the form of baskets as words, intending to explore and offer a compromise not so much between a long and short poem as culturally between free verse, metre and rhythm that inventively spice this kind of art. Yet, a poetic imagination that renews itself does not need to exclusively sacrifice its culture in the name of sheer objective pursuits. Rather than become a victim on all fronts, our cultural themes of research issue from and emphasize more the ideas that interplay simultaneously at both objective and subjective levels of cultural conceptualization, collection, communication and conservation within every communion of speakers and listeners, writers and readers of every age and place.

Closed, open or upside-down, each kola basket contains and explores ideas with a tenacity that depicts a rope with which a weaver plaits a basket or what keeps kola lobes together as a kola nut. As such, long and short sentences that express an idea equally depict ropes and shapes in words as baskets or kola nuts in form. Hence, readers and writers, as well as listeners and speakers can judge for themselves the imaginative conversations the author invites them to hear, read and share together, in the manner of kola fruits as each of the stanzas represents a basket of kola lobes, nuts, or pods, even if it is not always necessary to explicitly restate their eras, mentalities and places.

We present some words and expressions with or without a translation from a couple of Cameroonian and foreign languages. There is a glossary for those without a translation. Yet, a translation however perfect never fully escapes from what Italians proverbially depict as *traditor, tradittore!* This explains why our English translations complement what Albrecht Dürer (1471-1528), a German painter and engraver, did, when he wrote his work in German but under the Latin title of *Geometria Practica Nova.* Both of us, though separated by eras, disciplines, languages and traditions, if not continents, have similar but not identically complementary concerns. Together we draw attention to the relationship between a people's language and *a lingua Franca* like Latin and English, widely considered nowadays as global languages. But individually, a sole concern with mathematics differs from a poetry that draws attention to the mutual life of disciplines (Jeanne Peiffer: 1996 "La création d'une Langue mathématique allemande par Albrecht Dürer. La Raison de sa non Réception" in *Sciences et Langues en Éurope.* École des Hautes Études en Sciences Sociales (EHESS) Paris).

I remain indebted to many scholars, relatives and friends who have influenced me in one way or the other. My parents – Moósér Kíshaàne Yeèkpu Kòŋnyùy, my father, gave me a sense of dignity in life and sharpened my thirst for knowledge with a singular warmth of paternal concerns and love through his philosophical maxim of *Ghá' ke',* which verbally means: *beginning is difficult.* I derived my thirst for poetry from the songs, my mother, Regina Tanlaka Lámé-Taàlúkóŋ, used in driving away sleep from my eyes as she prepared banana envelopes of *mendóndó* during the late hours of the night for sale or cultivated yam farms just below what was known in colonial times as the Rest House at Bamkikà'ày, Kitiíwúm! Though I am grateful to all my relatives, brothers and sisters, I am particularly indebted to Dr. D. Moosúuka TanlaKíshaàni and Mr. P. Nyùydžěyuv Tanla-Kíshaàni whose encouragements kept me going in the course of writing the work. I also owe a lot to my babysitters who taught me oraural poems in my teens.

Mr. Maxillus Sɔ̀ndzə from Ŋkàr, nicknamed *Cícà Sòy,* my teacher in Infant Two opened my mind to the value of merit as he gave me a price of three pennies for successfully narrating a story in English at the St. Theresia's School, Kitiíwúm back in 1952. After a decade or so, as students and neophytes, our quenchless thirst for philosophy increased thanks to the clarity with which some of our philosophy Professors taught us. Precisely, at the Bigard Memorial Seminary, Enugu, Nigeria, one of our Professors, Rev. Fr. Kisane, an Irish of the Holy Ghost Congregation, left an indelible mark on our minds when he defined lying metaphysically as affirming non-being of being. As enthusiastic as we were about philosophy, well versed in it or not, we often engaged daily in prolonged philosophical debates in search for truth. Later on, we still, thanks to such programs as the Cameroon-Dickinson Exchange Program, enjoyed similar experiences at a wider range. Both Professor Emeritus George Allan, a contemporary USA philosopher and myself have shared and exchanged ideas since 1994. Mrs. Elizabeth Chilver, otherwise called Sally, brought me up in research both within the English literate traditions and the Cameroonian oraural norms. Many scientific researchers on Cameroon know her fondly as an *academic Mama fo tori*. I also owe a tribute to my students in the USA as well as to my numerous students at Yawunde University for almost three decades whose thirst for knowledge has spurred my research in Letters, Oraurality and Philosophy. I seize this opportunity to thank all of them.

At home, Professor Bernard Nso'kìka Fònlòn's entire life taught me that all is never lost even if things turn out gloomy and sad. Professor Daniel Noòne Là'ntum inspired me with the necessity of a locally based research. In the USA, Professor Christopher Wise, a friend and brother beyond words, wisely inspired me to write about kola nuts, as Professor Emeritus Milton Krieger, grandfather and elder brother, and Professor Judy Krieger, grandmother, have taught me that a friend is one indeed during the utmost needs of joy and sorrow. Dr. Paula Wagner of Wetter-Ruhr in Germany initiated me equally into the spoken and heard as well as the written and read, German before offering me a legacy that has kept me abreast with German scholarship in the pages of *Der Fels, Katholisches Wort in die Zeit*, since the 1980s. Rather a found but never lost mother, scholar and a source of inspiration since Christmas 1969, she died in 1996. Luckily then, I was in Europe and visited her remains at their family tomb in Wetter-Ruhr.

Matt Atwood and Alfred Vènsu, friends indeed, who carefully proofread the manuscript, merit a good kola nut to split and share. My son, Víshaàne Wiidìn Bòngáasu whose name of Víshaàne, if etymologically translated as Paschal, would have failed to retain the meaningful cultural and historical resonance it still has in Lamnso', deserves my paternal care and gratitude more than unmistaken words can describe. I owe him a lot more than his youthful age allows him to understand, though he alone knows the thick and thin through which we have had to undergo together. While I would like to encourage and inspire his future undertakings, I must still thank him for having inspired me as if on a daily basis with all I needed to write this poetic text whose imperfect nature I alone assume.

Poetry with a concrete cultural foothold neither shrinks from its universality nor from its particularity. The choice of our theme resulted from our desire to satisfy such a need. Reality belongs to and includes rather than solely cuts through the interstices of all disciplines. Our poetry explores the art of plaiting kola baskets of the cultures we experience at once as particular and universal. The universal that only defines itself by the common interstices of any reality, fails to satisfy the exigencies of concrete reality. Our poetry aims both at a change of mentality and the concrete practice of justice. Both of these as excessive magnanimity become as suspected as the extravagance, some practically set on the same footing to defend as bribery and corruption, one of the main (if not the inspiring) themes of *A Basket of Kola Nuts*.

I

Patterns of Kola Nut Baskets Upside-Down

"If a man comes to see you do you entertain him with crying? Get us something to entertain him. Bring a kolanut from the basket near my bed and give it to him."
Kenjo Jumbam: *The White Man of God* 1980 p. 150 1980 Heinemann

"Thank you. He who brings kola brings life."
Chinua Achebe: *Things Fall Apart* p. 5 (1958) 1972 Heinemann

"Then came September 11 – and Americans felt their world turned upside down... *Nous sommes tous Américains* (We are all Americans)."
Barack Obama: *The Audacity of Hope: Thoughts on Reclaiming the American Dream* pgs. 290, 292 2006 Crown Publishers

A Kola Nut of Life

A kola pod may hide in leaves
As in the undergrowth out of sight!
But its missionary task persists at heart,
As its first discoverer brings it into the fold,
Anew for fiends to shake hands with each other
As with peace plants in the friendship of the friend,
We've always spoken to you all about by name in bad
And good weather as we thrive intact from dawn to dusk!
He ever gives solace to everybody as insiders and outsiders,
At every second of our life here or beyond where a basket tilts
And turns at times as mirthfully as woefully upside-down within
The divine ear and eyeshot as with hands and nose of a mind we seek,
To so acknowledge Jesus as the friend in love, offering a new kola lobe
To all entities as a wholesome meal for every proverbial friend to share
In the universe full of woes and joys we no longer contain but sing out
Daily as: *Les choses qui arrivent aux autres commencent à m'arriver*!*

II

Ad Lib Kola Baskets

One splits and shares a lobe of kola nut,
Out of kindness with someone else, rather than
Out of selfishness! Such lone kola lobes weave ropes
Of endless conversations - even about the strong kola nuts,
We plant and crop, sort and eat as life's co-partners on earth!

For, like the truth,
Neither late nor early,
At home as well as abroad,
A nice kola nut too attracts all,
Though it's still puzzling to know
Why a kola fruit ever entices so much,
In spite of its bitter tastes and small sizes!
Why we plant to crop, sell and eat kola nuts!
Why the untold fame of kola nuts rubs shoulders
As if forever with utter bribery on altars as in embers,
We fuel to the brim with currencies of a mixed blessing!

In our daily bustle or sleep,
A dream shifts idleness aside,
As fingers keep an eye on crafts
And open a mind to basket making!
Like a basket weaver, I learn to weave
The hustle and bustle of kola into baskets!
I twist knitting aids under and over into plaits,
Networks or broody baskets of stark naked flames,
With the slippery hands of inborn patience and silence,
In a spicy den of wiles within a sanctuary of kola farms!

A kola lobe nourishes itself together
Within each single kola nut as a partner
In service, moulding the fold for its own part
Against every trick to tear living members apart
From the centres or pivots that grip kola in droves!
A kola lobe yokes wholesome in nuts of each kola pod
From birth as distinct but similar in their shape and size!
Yet, today kola nuts and kola pods buy and sell the birthrights,
They convert from their *in vivo* into the *in vitro* world of change!

A kola basketry spills over
Into a career of a red feather!*
A basket weaver plaits kola baskets
Of choice in beauty, name and strength
Out of bamboo, cane, elephant grass, palm,
And a fibrous rope that easily bends and twists
With the skills of hands as with the skills of minds
To dye and print the design that invites the eye-catcher
On roads that confer power to banana and plantain fibres,
A factory weaver now melts together with rubber to lengthen
The age-bracket of a basket's unique make up from birth to death!
A basket-worker weaves and produces a kola basket that'll ever carry
The kola fruits we crop to eat and sell rather out of pride than as bribes!

Every *bòbí naà wân*!*
Right or wrong, big or small,
It's ever more by taste than by size!
Since every species of kola nuts excels
In the kola tastes of its own unity in diversity,
A breast also feeds the wholesome truth of plurality
As one within many! Kola and breast-milk feed to cure!
Both the poor and the rich, men and women, young and old,
Today as of old, in secret or in public, eat kola fruits in chains!
Each handshake you exchange with kola nuts as pure gifts turns up
To openly, freely and fairly build bridges of family ties or encounters
That thrive in tested traditions of a people's timeless ethics to fight on
At every turn when alien handles of power break tragedies in the open!

We deck basketfuls of kola nuts out
In the finest banana leaves of each season,
To envelop the kola seeds we pack off in doubt!
We plant and crop to sell a kola fruit for its lesson!
Together we consume kola nuts for a thought that frees
Our souls and soils from cheating to embezzle public fees!
One throws the first stone* with a kola lobe to avoid a crime!
Though baboons believe themselves crimeless from their prime,
Crimeless monkeys toil as a sacrificial lamb for a criminal baboon!
For sanctity, saints till kola farms with guide dogs of virtue as a boon!

III

Baskets of Kola Nuts

Prologue

I

As *a lion's kola*,
A *bitter kola* earns,
A prize for excellence,
As the *átára nut* for twins,
Heirs and parents and rituals;
As a species of a *monkey's kola*,
One oft peels to eat without seeds,
Unlike the lobed kola nuts many share
To eat with every variety of kola pepper,
One relishes for its unsalted peppery dishes!
People cherish kola with names like *bíy*, **goorò**,
Oft, in spite of the abusive role it plays as *ŋgòmbò*!
A kola nut spices life for mutual consumers in bunches!
Unlike the intimate universe one carries about but in a bag,
Once crowned as *res publica*, kola nuts thrive at best in baskets!

Amidst daily wars as woes and joy as peace,
Faces and hands meet to laugh and weep!
In kindred greetings with a kola nut,
One tickles the fancy of a happy giver!
Adults like to share and chew a kola nut,
As thirsty children share to eat groundnuts,
Berries, biscuits and sweets to quench a thirst!
One who eats kola nuts also needs to sow a seed,
For the newly born to crop, eat or sell after seasons
Of unspoken memories of a dream few discern to crop
From the dusty locks of kola tombs, riddles or proverbs!
Today we still bank kola nuts of a by-gone planter or tiller!
Wiser consumers of kola nuts till and sow kola seeds that feed
Members of the UN General Assembly in a full rainbow session!
In a bid to perpetuate the mission of the *kìkéŋ* peace plant to grow,
We crop, share and eat our kola lobes for golden dreams to come true!
Justice as injustice still thrives within a lot of human minds and senses!

9

II

A loyal omen,
As her royal sign,
Still outshines today,
Bright and fresh at birth,
Rather like the morning star!
By spider divination as by design,
She eclipses live myths, full of mirth!
A Prime Maiden still at her pilgrim's bar,
Already graces and hails the rainbow to x-ray
Our lost voices with pairs of kola parings plus one!
Let a fragrant peace plant safely guide her steps home!
Palm wine and kola nuts marry in seasons untold in Rome!
One crowns the cowry bowl of age on her laps as in her hands,
With the cam-wood and red oil that quietly trap a thief on the run!
For Salvation, a thief fought tooth and nail to repent and gain the land!

Oft, a kolaly divination still protects,
A hand of an artistic ambuscade it detects!
In our absence, others still exchange kola nuts,
As a loyal fruit for all, born in purple and in chains!
Beyond hunger and thirst we share and chew kola lobes!
We praise *Mbií-Fòn* and *Ŋwéròŋ* as we long for kola nuts!
A kola search rivals winds like *Bàrà'* in search of knowledge!
Kola tastes uncover within eye or earshot in baskets as in books!
O Maiden of kola homes! A kola tree or pumpkin growing by brooks
Whets our taste, as the tick-tocks of home spittle-clocks dry on a ledge
We ritually sweep to dust in a plight of the voiceless to weep over fate!

The world changes in the single seeds,
A kola tree yields and knots as the classics,
One crops with thanks within nature's garden!
Kola trees ever yield kola nuts with the kola peels,
One takes off to divine, share and eat to kick up heels!
As the civics of slavery or the moral victims of its burden,
Now take a new turn to foster the duty to set every slave free,
Slaves of fashion in body and mind change hands like kola seeds!
A unique rate of a new exchange now spins out of control with glee,
As a proverbial dream of Jesse's tears ushers in Obama's open politics!

III

A basket also serves a weaver and a user to cage every kind of fowl!
In case a kola trader sells kola and buys a gwàgwá to rear at home,
A *should-in-case* basket one brings along always carries the day!
One covers a mother hen and chickens at night with a basket!
Oft, we lock up a hen that sucks all its eggs under a basket!
One carries hens, chickens and cocks about in a basket!
But, we chose to carry the universe rather in a bag!

Once a kola trade mushrooms a market at the church door,
It surely sets things upside-down, as attendants increase,
In a way that oft outnumbers most regular churchgoers,
As basket weavers begin to expect rather more gains,
A user in need offers for each chosen kola basket!
But once, a kola trade mushrooms a new market
Within the heavenly gate, churchgoers, traders
And weavers will all set everything upright,
For one prefers a share in heavenly gains!
The holy seek, trade and weave in faith
To win but what no longer corrupts,
Like a kola nut everyone breaks
Wholeheartedly in generosity
Along a pilgrim's step!

A basket of kola nuts used to barter for a calabash of oil,
Between loyal kola nut and palm-oil traders, basket weavers
And calabash designers, dividing a call into basketry, designing,
As trade patterns of choice, home painters design on hats and mats,
As women, skillfully balancing a full basket or calabash on the head!
A kola nut one shares enables the head to balance works of art in life!

A carver shapes a broken calabash as a painter designs
A bamboo kẃrákwàrà with the *gàlúrí* for an eye-catcher!
A wood-carver makes chairs and doors for leaders and peoples,
To eschew crops of kola nuts with every timely cup of palm-wine,
To call on the gods of ancestors to split kola and spit a kind blessing
For the living dead from *Ŋgòŋ* as for every new-born into life or death!

Baskets of Kola Nuts

1

At its best,
A modest exchange
Of our handshake, blest
With a kola nut, pod or seed,
Often calls for the mutual sharing
Of our life's joys and sorrows, our cry
And our laughter! As an omen and a token,
A catalyst and a stimulant of success and failure,
An offer of a kola nut often opens all kinds of roads
We take to walk at once in life like trickles down cheeks,
Clothes we wear over the head and stick arms out sideways,
Or legs down-wards from pairs of shorts and trousers into shoes!
A bitter kola soon sweetens as we share and chew a lobe together!

By sheer love,
Each nice kola nut,
We break here to divide,
Chip in our opinions together,
Or nod a welcome to bid a farewell
In silence and words, lobbies and rallies
Human wits at best into a daily communion
Of kola wayfarers for road safety at every step!

For, in nature's face,
Always single or manifold,
But, fully intact in its interface
Of choice and kind, the kola gold
We mete out, cheers to unify a partaker
With a vivid grip on body and soul together!
Nature's kola nut ever numbers its lobes or pods
With unique varieties of colour, smell, size and taste
That woo the mind with a fine touch to speak in a tongue
Of no accents to other consumers both indoors and outdoors!
It takes an agent to plant, but a village's world to eat a kola nut!
As honest partakers expect to win rather than to corrupt a kind gift,
The kola nut we offer heals to uphold peace in its golden handshake!

Once at hand,
An integral kola nut wins
An idler's negligent ear or eye
To set the mind at work, but oils
A worker's elbows to feed the mind!
A tasty kola re-echoes through the tasks
We pursue to drudge at a call until we win!
The kola nut a child, a father and a mother digest
As members of a city's household, will in turn bind
Other friendly birds of a feather with its salivary taste!
A house of *Ŋwéròŋ* or *Ŋgírì* may never eschew bitterness,
But, a house of love enkindles to chew all in a shared kola nut!
As basic etiquette or a first step to shun sloth, a youth at heart toils
To pick a kola for an elder and freely gain an upper hand in sharing!

As an elixir to cure
Hearts with love and turn
Foes more into friends, an offer
Of a kola pod we handpicked, blesses
With a giver's firm grip of smiles to knot
The grace of love over the disgrace of crimes!
Offenses idly mask markets of gossip to wheedle
Shepherds of love into a bid of offhand murmuring
Over what still curses the guilt of the guilty in silence!

2

To offer a kola nut blesses
The warmth of a guest's welcome!
Quite often, a worthy kola nut upholds
The giver's mettle within its size and taste!
A fruit with open arms, the tiny kola we offer,
Still covers a pocketful, a handful or a basketful!
An offer of a big or small kola zigzags laws of merit
In its size as in its taste! Slippery or not, we credit both!
We praise the will to offer kola in a basketful as in a pod!
The kola nut we share mirrors an inner unity of its flavour!
Our proverbial *Mbàcà' dzò mvóm*: Cymbals ring like the mite
Of a widow that glitters rather from within than from without!
Taste measures a good kola nut as content mirrors a good book!
We never judge a kola nut by the shape of kola pods or kola trees!

Hence, our dynasties,
Like time, ageless but young,
Daily tick and sprout within ruins
Of jaws and bowels of a kola forest,
We nestle in the fat arms of virgin soils,
A centuries-godly host still flush with crops
And cash-eclipses of mossy mushroom homes!
We nurse kola laws and norms, intact as in tatters
To renew all with freedom and justice on a daily basis,
As we fumble to mend our free way and intone kola songs,
We rate as fit relics for the lone morrow's miraculous game!
Like time we till our kola trees of proverbial heroes and heroines,
With our ethnic anthem of the legendary founders and foundresses
Like *Kìmè, Mbàm, Ncaàrì Yéèŋ and Ŋgòn Nso'* famed for their risk
On the sad cliff of kola trade to tip values that tell fortune for safety!

So ex officio,
As potent as it's chaste,
And as familiar as it's alien,
Our simplest gift under the sun,
A modest kola nut inside or outside
Trees, pods and peels, in age and name,
In rain and sun, promises mortals no moon!
Freely honest without a sigh in anybody's guess,
An offer of a kola pledges a richer turn of kindness!
Spoken tongues rich in jargons and wise in laws suckle
To spread influenza in kola faiths, firms, rules and tongues
With a lone hand in concert with their rivals the world-over!
A wanton elite knits up its strange basketry of bribery and lust
With sly kola nuts of foul plays to disarm a farm of its lush arms
In old kola fields we daily shield within the dust and din of rituals,
As alien to us as prone to lay a liable fire to inflame pet with pride!
Daily, injuries of insult sprout as flashy as wit with audio-visual aids
Of the filthy piracy, blossoming at random as unabated as unabashed,
At home and abroad with new spoils of office as a medicinal kola nut!
A sham crusader easily milks to impoverish the poor by a mock charity
That hand-crops kola fruits to turn a lusty kola tree into dry kola wood!
Wind-driven parasites as in baskets of lies sway kola markets for good!

Today unlike of yore,
Newly woven kola baskets
Turn upside down, inside out
And tear, as kola trees of fortune
Shrivel up the blessings of rich fruits,
Anointed from within to uplift with grace,
Rather than to slander and hurt from without
With an untried arrow of crime as error's crown
Of a bitter taste and an open disgrace! A wily talent
Freely bribes to corrupt with sly kola bites! Kola fruits
Tie a child, father and mother together in the egg of a home
As members of a civil family nursing oneness in many or many
In oneness to enkindle the love of toil and outbid palms of idleness
With those kola arms of justice bartering gifts of home-grown crops
For endless generations with all the master keys of a mutual pursuit!

Oft, like the languages,
We speak and spread at home
In our world of a mental captivity,
We also sell kola nuts in baskets to share
The tasks of consumption with alien consumers!
With a kola nut at hand to assuage an orphan-mind,
We weave baskets and mats of memories too to honour
Heroic names of a variety of other peoples, places and eras,
We rewrite as Sóv, *Támnyàm* or *Bòkídé'*, *Yoolà* or *Wèrìmaayò*,
Whither footing and riding on kola donkeys, we carried foot-loads
To chase off donkey-loads to ride new kola cars, lorries and planes!

3

An example
From childhood,
Knits its lessons up
From our teens as an era
Of rich kola harvest and trade,
When father or mother took turns
To bundle leafy baskets of kola seeds
We treasured under bamboo beds to whet
Our appetite and draw the smiles of a guest,
Mirroring kola woods like every kind of jewel
That glitters backwards to the heavens in sunshine!

Quite often,
As our daily bread
In those days, as young
And energetic as ever-caring,
Mother would offer a sugar cane,
Cocoon the best corn loaves and yams,
In meal baskets to nourish a morrow's game,
As on market days father foraged with kola nuts,
To bring home some rarer kinds of precious delicacies
Like *dàvàdává, shirùm, fish, groundnuts and new sweets*
To tickle our lessons of *book* to grow like kola in kola trees!
Thus, we grew on the soft laps of a father and a mother's care,
Still nursing to share the kola nuts they planted to crop with age!

And now what glitters
From our abiding memories
As a kola seed of a life's light,
Still gathers generations that'll live
To share their ritual life of mutual laws
With shields of love beyond our boundaries!
A public tree like the old hand *kiyínsam* kola tree,
Ancestors planted to fight flash hunger at crossroads,
As nobody's property even feeds passers-by both on tiptoe
And at will without ever claiming or disclaiming its ownership!
Ever as green in its foliage, full in its tillage as steel in its growth,
The old hand takes road charity off the soiled hands of utter bribery!

Though almost forgotten,
My own memories flow still
From early success in first exams!
Father never congratulated most of us,
As teachers, neighbours and villagers did,
With showers of greetings in chorus as friends
And relatives! Father exchanged but handshakes
With a thrilling well-wisher, a friend and relatives,
As his big head-load, a full *kaáyá*, turned and set out
With kola donkeys and neophytes for *Yoolà* and beyond,
To trade for book fees and the delicacies of mother's beads!

Yes oft, I saw
Father shaking hands,
To exchange a nice kola nut
Of comfort, before he left home,
With a guest, a neighbour or relative,
And wish a richer annual harvest of crops
In faith with the clear voices of wise kola peels,
He had prayed to grant all kinds of fortune's justice
As he began to weave ropes of conversations to prompt
A kola nut to restore a bunch of impromptu justice and laws
To age on like a new kola tree we'd planted to sustain our lives!
My kola trees are but your mothers, sisters, brothers and relatives!
Oft, father would tip us by the fireside, in coffee farms and elsewhere!

4
One day,
Father surprised us,
Brother, sister and myself,
With some wholesome kola seeds,
He gave each of us to plant on the ruins
Of a house he built in youth and owned in life:
Once you're of age with schooling or no schooling,
With a trade or no trade, at home or abroad, you'll crop!
Let your great ambitions ever grow taller than tall kola trees!

Thus,
Within groups
Of teens we aged on,
Moving from era to era,
And from school to school
At home and in far-off lands,
On desert shores as on seashores!
Once father and mother entrusted me
With tatters of leafy packets of kola nuts,
As rare, well-tried and proven as weevil free
And undying in the knotty strings of silent norms,
To take as a better voucher to sell and live by auction,
And eke out the livelihood of *my book*, since the evil hands
Of theft had untimely-deprived Daddy of a glimmer of fortune!

With a surprising,
And yet timely gesture,
Mummy silently chipped in
Her rare chunk of unique savings,
She had surely gathered from the sales
Of home-grown and home-made delicacies
Like baskets of kola nuts, loaves of *foofoo corn*
And leafy rolls of *mendóndó*, enveloped to win styles
Into extra-smoked banana leaves and trade by wholesale!
Oft mother earned and saved her treasures on a daily basis
From the meager sales of nature's broken and unbroken pods
Of handpicked kola at home in rain or sun, at dawn or at sunset,
From beneath full-grown women's crops seasoned in men's fields!
We hanker after the footstep of parents to drudge at book-delicacies!

As a mother's precious gift,
A kola nut free from tricky aims,
In joy and in sorrow, truly consoles!
I now hail both with a kola grain of glee
As we revive a full litany of all relic-helpers,
We yodel and beckon by eponyms across planets,
Rich in scary experiences and ruled by bare chance!
We grace bravery with the priceless kola lobe of solace
In careers that beam high in the blue skies of a fine victory,
But ail and fade within hail into pure regrets of a sole failure!
Big and small, young or old, we pay everyone a tribute by name
As we set forth bulky calabashes of mellow palm-wine and share
Kola nuts of taste from left to right as from women to men by right
Of old customs and new conquests to free everyone - body and soul!
As our twin ingredients of growth or great allies of choice, one pays
A tribute first to parents, babysitters and teachers at home or abroad!
We exhort *Nyùy Mbóm* to enlighten and bless them to share our gifts
Of a cock, kola and palm-wine in token of the best to dispel despair!
We set the pace on ancestral heels to free the chain-stitch of bribery,
And dust off body and mind to nurse sanctity with the salves of kola
And soothe all with a great effort of will in and out of home or land!
On time we canonize a Martin Luther King, Jr. or a John F. Kennedy,
Once afflicted with rheumatic dreams to undo every abuse of power!

So, while we pray
In Latin, Deo Gratias,
In Arabic, *Salaam Alekum*,
Or in Hebrew, *Yahweh Shalom*,
To pour wine to *Nyùy Mbóm* at home,
Before the inmost prying eyes of a believer,
We all gather within our island of benediction,
With a singular grain of due thanks by the armful,
To sow kola nuts here or there, harvest and trade off
Each new basket of injustice to forgive every trespasser
And pay tribute to heroes and heroines with peace plants
Such as a Mahatma Gandhi or a Nelson Mandela at hand!

Quite often,
When nobody cares,
A full seedling of *a thank-you*,
As a memorial bag of the kola nuts,
We crop to share now and again by hand,
Divines a random loss of forgotten gratitude,
To renew the sympathy we once nursed at heart!
It sustains countless medicinal fruits from kola trees,
To emerge with new cotyledons of our life's sole commerce
To pour out the unspeakable truth within a recycling communion!
The least kola nut we duly share heals at best within a conversation!

As sympathetic and kind
As the kola gift we give or take
With the open-arms of a *thank-you*,
Kola nurses bitterness into sweetness!
The longer one chews a nice kola seed over,
The sweeter its taste outstrips to refresh weariness,
Heal hunger and enliven all the stories of human lives!
The boomerang of a kola offering echoes in a million ways!
So, fortune comes with a peaceful gift of an even kola number
As kola lobes in a kola nut or kola nuts in their kola pods!
We carry the world in a bag, but kola seeds and pods
In airy baskets, we deck with leaves to outnumber
Their chameleon age-brackets quality ways!

A harbinger of fortune,
Kola feeds on the breast of lands!
A receiver shares a giver's aggregate kola,
As full medicine in body and mind that uproots
Pure weariness to implant virtue and whisper hope!
Oft, kola tickles lies with sympathy even among thieves!
Kola betrays a rare presence in the hide-and-seek of thieves,
Once it turns sweet in the best hideout, thieves proverbially laugh!
So we chew it over as:*Wen tru tori de swit, tif man de laf fo banda!
Agents of bribery and corruption fear the sweet kola lobes of justice!

5

Alone,
But at times,
Also in company,
A kola nut that breaks
A lucky day's silent order,
Drops down at dawn or at noon,
And turns the youths crazy in search
Of fresh, big and small pods of kola nuts,
To pick out as a vocational kola fruit in life!
An unsoiled pod, seed or lobe of kola may turn up
As plaintive as grips of greetings from prodigal hands,
That'll soon gladden the heart of every *primus possedentis*!
We shade drops of tears in joy, once we spot a fallen kola pod,
Broken or unbroken, but cropped from the holy hands of nature!
If in youth we offer childless parents kola and daily drops of water,
In old age we price calabashes of palm-wine with art tastes for kola!

Kola trees grow best
On the ruins in our homes,
In plains and valleys and hills!
Our curtain of kola trees gropes on
Freely on hilly slopes or windy fields,
To yield cartloads of wholesome kola seeds,
We trade along spiral footpaths of market-farms,
We nurse and narrate in aging stories of kola songs,
How we buy and sell with the kola head-loads we carry!

More often than not,
As we sell lobed kola nuts,
Travelling on foot and on rails
As in alien cars, planes and ships,
A bitter kola nut quenches our thirst
And tips, thrills and reconciles friends
And foes beyond the best price that mirrors
The drift of value in colour, mass, size and taste!

So, out of hunger and thirst,
We often exchange handshakes,
With a kola nut to bless a journey
And season greetings of a farewell!
A kola nut seasons a family reunion!
A kola nut still blesses every wedding
With good omens of kola shells and pods
As couples grow from silver to diamond age!

The kola we share, knots and bars
One from digging one's future grave!
A kola prepares and hands over such a task
To kola partakers after the deluge of one's life!
For alive but dying, one digs one's grave out of fear
To leave a lobed kola seed for one's future grave-diggers,
Who'll by chance bury one's body like Joseph of Arimathea!

Like a person
We name to call
Always by a name,
Kola trees ever flourish
With lay names from tender
To old age and the life beyond,
As they fail now to succeed after,
Or even succeeding here to fail there!
Kola tills every root of a true friendship,
And spices our lives with its smiles of love!
Kola cajoles the sorrows of injustice into sleep,
As we chew kola lobes to dribble hunger and thirst!

As a fine catalyst
Of adult conversation,
A genuine offer of a kola nut
We break, share together and chew,
Titillates and turns smiles into laughter!
One may shed tears out of strain and stress!
A kola nut opens roads for smiles and laughter,
Once it oils palms to limit tipster foes and friends!
A voice of kola best cheers up a dusty palm with hopes
As it dries up trickles of tears with pure laughter and jokes
To poke all in the ribs where one elbows ways by kola nut tips!
At best kola converts an evil, controls gossip and turns anger into care!

One or many,
Both big and small,
Fresh and old kola seeds,
Whitish and pinkish kola nuts
Together, tag after the same name!
Single or plural in pods and in shapes,
Lobed kola nuts grow together like fingers!
Fingers beckon and befriend almost in silence
To win the vicious over to become the virtuous,
As they forgive their best unforgivable life-stories!

A kola fruit brings
Life to grow peacefully!
We share a kola nut to fight,
In the name of justice together,
Against the injustice of corruption!
A kola nut strengthens an honest life,
As it straightens the fraud of the greedy
And the vicious who only outwardly claim:
'Behold my kola nut I'd like to share with you!'
A kola nut at hand fits both the just and the unjust!
A gift of a kola nut, intact or broken, may woo a thief
To repent before the wiser *Njò'-voices* of kola pods speak
And unveil crafty embezzlers who bribe to corrupt in silence!
A kola nut of deceit tends to lame the peacemaker and the just!
Yet, a fine kola gathers consumers into a communion of friends!

6

To share a friend's kola nut
Also sweetens the taste of dialogue!
A kola tree around a house shields a home!
Counting kola nuts teaches the arts of numbering!
Kola lobes by nature mirror a full rainbow of justice
And set the pace for all, big or small, to discuss together!
Every species of kola nuts in its foliage, lobes, pods and trees,
Mirrors touchy bonds of rare traditions, tongues and philosophies!

Always by birth
Every leopard comes
With spots into the world!
Kola trees by nature also beget
A kola pod in time with kola nuts!
Today's legacies of wise earth-spiders
Uphold the insight of spider-legged weeks,
The prying eight hundred eyes of the *Fon* echo,
As the even lobes of kola nuts beget good fortune!
A day's question to vote on gender ever hints names,
For boys and girls wisely in favour of unerring justice!
So, we still divine the married knot of a quorum of seven
When the *Fon*'s college rules on the basis of sheer fairness!
For, big or small, kola lobes do not fight for size in a kola nut!
In and out, every kola lobe reigns as one in many or many in one
Kola fruits of justice by nature ever outstrip the powers of bribery!

Always, like a stitch
In its own time to save nine,
Every lobed kola by far stitches
Every order of honesty with justice
To crown kola nuts as the *king of fruits*!
Often each kola tree serves notice in silence
And edifies our lips and teeth to chew all over
For love to undo the zips of the rich and the poor!
A kola nut unites all under a banner of the life we share!
With the kola nut at hand everyone forgives to forget at heart!

Yet, to plant a kola seed
We'll harvest, takes a while!
To share a kola nut gladdens hearts!
To split a kola pod to divide lasts a wink!
Edible kola nuts open the blood ties of nature
To build couples of nations by dint of soothsaying
With the divining *Njò'-parings* we number in the plural,
To espy with four eyes how kola nuts do turn hearts purer!

Small in size,
Rich in caffeine,
Kola nuts taste bitter!
At one's own sweet will,
Pinkish and whitish in kind,
A kola nut sweetens in its choice!
The flawless shape of each kola seed,
Like each single lobe keeps justice intact!
Many in order and taste, all kola fruits season
Rituals of life as condiments to open and crown
A birth with a welcome and a death with a farewell!
Kola oils live-dialogues with tasty cupfuls of palm wine!

7

Like people around,
Kola trees also flourish
To perish within an age-span!
Kola trees change hands and names!
Kola fruits follow the fashion of new rivals
Like the factory coffee and tea we harvest and dry
On *kwárákwàrà* mats or bamboo baskets to sell in kind!
Modern baskets of our making and style now openly fight
Shy of plastic papers within a new freedom of origin and use!
With new aims, we carry kola nuts, carrots, coffee, groundnuts,
Pepper, potatoes, tea or tobacco far and wide in search of markets!
Kola often roves over seas and lands, up and down or left and right,
Where fellows of a school in uniforms steal a march on time's laws!
Many a shape and style of kola home-plaited baskets rot willy-nilly,
As archaic, dirty, empty, fragile or silent ash-bins set to blaze away
As rival, neat, light, cheap, plastic papers reign by day and by night!

Today out of sheer love
For the give-and-take of kola nuts,
One easily falls a prey to a party politics,
Or wry policies in a shambles of self-reliance!
Hand-works of basketry escape insects and mice!
Dressed in leaves, baskets with lids refresh kola nuts,
Unlike packets of tea-leaves, sweets, coffee, cigarettes,
Bottles and tins of beer, grain or oil, a rival factory parcels
With an expiring date of grace into plastic papers at extra costs!
A live lobe of kola nut doctors alcoholics, but enlivens workaholics!
We spice to revive kola nuts in baskets of banana or plantain leaves!

Thus, refreshing
In nature's envelopes,
With its flavour of innocence,
Within breezy, cool, leafy baskets,
A kola seed stores its aroma in nature!
We basket kola in leaves to suckle its age,
And leap in a dark road of danger or despair!
A life comes with *nothing venture, nothing gain*!
Be the owners bad, sad or mad, *at-home* is a palace!
Arm in arm strands of smoke stroll into the cloudy sky!
A lonely rat in a house returns to the fold as tears of fear
Often well up and drop down into the trickles of by-streams
To flow far, fast or slow in droves as rivers, seas and oceans!
Far from home or near, the joys of a welcome pour out to settle
With the handshakes we exchange to strip, split and eat kola nuts
In a medley of folksongs we weave at the lyric peak of a dialogue!
We bind the stillborn, the unborn, the living, the dying and the dead
Together in a communion of life's wayfarers Ŋgòn Nso' still gathers
As she strays afar or near, in shame or with pride, at home or abroad
By the power of chance as by the experiences of design! All ears and
Eyes await a safe homecoming, alive or dead, O Sojourn Ŋgòn Nso'!
Return afresh like a daily trail of smoke from your straggling village!
Ŋgòn Nso'! Come as a trickle of hope with its full sense of direction!

Á kó' tén, á kfər mbàŋ!
Mo á sán bíy, á mà' njò'!
One first reaps a palm tree,
To chew some palm kernels,
As one first breaks a kola nut,
To ably divine with kola peels!
A kola nut we break to share together
And chew, either breaks our yes from our no,
Or immensely weds a fitting no to a blest yes!

O royal sojourner of Màŋkìm!
Begotten free under a seal of loyalty
As an alert and nameless daughter of Nso'!
Our dazzling tigress that bestirs from top to toe,
With royal graces in the clean waters of wiser eyes
As with the fee necklaces and the earrings of our choice!
A spotless beauty in the finest strings of new cowries-pearls,
We anoint to redress and recycle with full cut-bowls of palm-wine,
She caresses to carry on filial laps with serene hands laden with a kola
And the peace plants to retrace the prodigal step of yore in the dew of youth,
As our drums and flutes cheer up the homecoming of more ageless ritual icons!
Rituals in ritual out we yearly secure a right of way back home as from a home!
With the blessings of raindrops still pouring to coo yea and wed seas, soils, stars
And all we rebuild to build and oil to age on in our cam-wood crown of destiny!

Ŋgòn Nso' stirs in stirring times!
Once stranded in youth to bequeath
A tender seedling and plant a token kola
Under the sway of Màŋkìm, she flourished
And never faltered as an off shoot in full moon!
She ventured in strict confidence to fly ever higher
Than all birds in feather into the skies of big ambitions,
And sink deeper as the best rival of lively ants and worms
That nurture all the living dead within the core-sheets of soils,
Away from white ants and sharp spears of thunder and lightning!
Abreast centuries her statue outwits flawless arrays of sun and rain
With which the holy hands of *Nyùy Mbóm* ply to guide the universe!
With a yearly sacrifice of cam-wood, fowls, kola nut and palm-wine
We scan ears and eyes to prune top kola secrets at the flash of dawn!

Ŋgòn Nso'! Once moved to tears
In search of thicker blood than water!
Bemused, we bemoan but the loss of all
On hills, plains and valleys! *Ee Yéèŋ wor á!*
Bitter sobs as of yore! *Ee Yéèŋ wor á, àá Yéèŋ!**
Swell up with palm wine! *Ee Yéèŋ wor á, àá Yéèŋ!*
Gigantic, cocks tether goats! *Ee Yéèŋ wor á, àá Yéèŋ!*
Ŋgòn Nso'! Daughter of Màŋkìm! Camwood of destiny!
Maiden of bosom blossoms! An idiomatic mother of Nso'!
A lily as radiant as the peace plant we till from farm to farm
To replant like the legendary kola tree we always reap and sow
In anxiety to simply retell a simple story of lost emblems of art!
Ee Yéèŋ wor á, àá Yéèŋ! Ee Yéèŋ wor á, àá Yéèŋ! Ee Yéèŋ wor á!
Kifú ké wìr kee mò Nyùy-iì kursin ne, lá wìr yò' wìy wày kiwó sho!
Let nobody set hands into somebody's leaf that God already knotted!

O Maiden cleansed from oblivion!
Shwà' yii layì, á wàa tà' vité' vidzɘm!
We fetch a lost knife in every framework!
Wàn yii layì, á yéné, á kaànè e kibam ke fíy ki!
We welcome a lost but found child with a new bag!
Ŋgòn Nso'! Rather than rain, skies swell up eyes to pour
But our dirges! *Ee Yéèŋ wor á, àáYéèŋ! Ee Yéèŋ wor á, àá!*
Ŋgòn Nso'! Astir in presence or absence! *Ee Yéèŋ wor àá, àá !*
Vèr Yéèŋ kì dù bóy á, àá Yéèŋ! Ee Yéèŋ wor á, àá Yéèŋ! Ee Yéèŋ!
Together, Yéèŋ and I went to trap tadpoles! *Ee Yéèŋ wor á, àá Yéèŋ!*

8

Oo Gracious God you see*
What the white man did hm, hm, hm!
When they first came here hm, hm, hmmm!
They gave us looking glasses hm, hm, hm, hmm!
Then they said to us, let us go to their ship hm, hm!
Hm, hm, hm, hmmm! Hm, hm, hmmm! Hm, hm, hmmm!
When we got to their ship, they took their guns and said!
Get on board, you black man Negro! Get on board! Hm hm!
You think I'm joking! Get on board! They started to shout and so
They rowed away, into Canaan rowed away! Still they rowed away!
When they died, they threw them overboard! Still they rowed away!

*You told me**
You'd meet me
At the station gate!
How long must I wait
For you? Jingo Jang Jazz
Is a solemn jazz that makes
Our heart to be four feet five!
Hipi Yipi! Hipi Yipi! Habap Hap!
Hipi Yipi! Yip Yip Yip Habap Hap!

Ŋgòn Nso'! *Wann und wo,*
*Sehen wir uns wieder und sind froh?**
Worn down on the footpaths of adventure
And ransomed from the royal ashes of rivalry
To elope willy-nilly into the odd arms of loyalty,
A whistle-stop of *Glauning's SOS* whipped you off
In droves as vain ritual emblems to retrace the spoors
Of slave caravans under the hidden clouds that open out
As weather-bound as mute with ages of their wintry smiles
To bid above the highest kola bidding! Ŋgòn Nso' outshine!
**Mein Hahn ist todd! Mein Hahn ist todd! Mein Hahn ist todd!*
Er kann nicht mehr singen Krokodil, Krokus dein! Er kann nicht!

Ŋgòn Nso', outshine!
To offer a kola nut is golden!
Every kola, big or small, forgives
The unforgivable and opens new roads
Into homes of single hearts with no snares,
For better and for worse as by dint of good will!
A kola pod falls in rain and shine as a knotted leaf!
A kola nut for *Baàbá, yaàyà yóò! Maàmá, yaàyà yóò!**
Brings every child up within the bosom arts of a kola gift
In every Baàbá olée! Yaàyà yóò! *or Maàmá* olée! Yaàyà yóò!
Daady welcome! I picked two fat half-cracked kola pods at noon!
Is that so! Where're they? Near the bed! I've now four basketfuls!
Hello! Mummy welcome! Maàmá olée! Yaàyà yóò! Maàmá Yaàyà!
Baàbá olée! Yaàyà yóò! Maàmá olée! Yaàyà yóò! Baàbá Olée Yaàyà!
Mummy! Let me carry the bigger bag! It is too heavy! What is inside!
Nothing else but daily joys and sorrows of kola fruits in stirring times!

Maàmá olée! *Yaàyà yóò*!
Mummy! Sá'nyùy picked kola pods-
Two fat kola pods from the *Bíy Kimbàŋ* tree!
Please, give me some to eat! That tree tastes nice!
It tastes like the stories of its growth at *kiwóoy ke bíy*!
Mummy! We went there searching somewhere else in vain!
Then, Sá'nyùy raised an alarm as he picked the first one! Again
Down a crackling noise, *kpìm*! Right before him a cracked pod!
Daady's call for dishes! Bàá! Here's a knotty leaf of kitchen meat!
We'll soon break full kola pods and peel the kola nuts to bundle up
Into a donkey's basket and knotted leaves for every service at home
And every sell abroad as we feed and drill all Jack-and-Jenny asses!

A ready kola pod autographs
A unique signature on kola branches
And leaves like hailstone, with a crackle
That crashes down *kpìm* to roll away *shwaà*
On dry leaves to a stop, awake like a chameleon,
In all weather until a discoverer will rescue to chew,
Offer and sell as a tasty kola from the *Bíy Kimbàŋ* 'tree,
Now a marketable name for kola fruits, 'elders' call *Bíy way*,
A been-to adult, Bíy yeé *Pànyá*, young traders, *Kaáyá woó Gèmbú*,
As stories change hands from zealous expeditions toward new icons!

Once at home,
Or away from home,
We exchange kola nuts,
Still to converse about home
And every life away from home,
That recalls life in and out of home!
Kola nuts and palm wine recall songs,
Like the old-timer of *Home again, again,*
One usually sings at home or abroad in need
Of a home at heart or there where we're at home
To work at night as from daybreak to achieve a goal
And still feel at home with alien home-works of tongues,
We now speak at home with homespun kola nuts of choice!
After a nostalgic stay from a kola home, it's good to be home!

Shaà cér aá wàá lo!
Caà ceé aá vaàvàá lo!
Forward quickly let's go!
With a small basket of kola
To continue on where I breathe
Little by little to breathe no more!
Elders live a life before they leave it
For the youth to forget or to remember,
And forgive and live better than they lived!
Wónlĕ ndzev á wàá lo! Caà ceé áa vaàvàá lo!
To fetch water mornings or evenings from streams
We search for fallen kola pods under fruity kola trees!
At times we grope still on all fours step by step like babies,
At times we babble excitedly in tongues to fight it out together!

9

Century after century,
Torn between royal stools
With their matchless eponyms
In tongues a pacesetter once bore
Maternally, as full kola legacies up
And down the foot-paths of hills, plains
And valleys of choice within desert-shores,
Where the tattooed zebra seals an eye-catcher
Within a land's zebra crossings of Ŋwéròŋ staffs,
To rally eyes more out of pure curiosity than priority
Of ownership, and rebind every parental umbilical cord,
We now sever from an incognito sojourn into the Berlin walls,
To yell out an SOS for bosom ones to clutch at all straws of hopes,
We wield stately *gongs* and peace plants there with the Ŋwéròŋ staffs
To quicken the homecoming of both the enslaved and lost effigies of arts,
And yearn for a smudge of the unspoken kola tattoos on the taboos of hopes!

Ŋgòn Nso'!
Within Ethiopia
Awake and blossom!
The Berlin Wall yawns,
As our bosom effigies cry,
And cry aloud for time to dry
Their tears and rely on souvenirs
Of worlds apart ready in the offing!
As the Fon's royal summons crops up
To bind all with a handy ŋwéròŋ's staff,
Vows of dialogue stray beyond the Cold War,
To forgive more than to forget the rash dividends
Of African art, the Berlin Wall freezes in alien snow!
Yet, time spells a new elopement back home from shame
With a sense of pride in a kola nut handshake of forgiveness!

33

Once more at home,
The *Afo-a-kom* stirs a few
Loamy truths home to avert anew,
Tactfully stolen kola wands of fine arts,
We embrace with charismatic coins of darts,
Wholly frozen stiff at the eleventh hour to frown
At a divide-and-rule or square an implant-and-own,
As the tricks of policies one needs to cut down to size!
A crown gains or loses to mend its fences in order to rise,
Rather than loot and plunder works of art for fame's crown!
Sacred waters bless the ritual shrines within older kola forests
With the divine breath of harmony in nature's heart by a design!
At home seasons of kola fruits mirror clay-mats we carve as maps,
On which heads of cattle foot together up and down to drill and sign
A choice a youth drudges on unabatedly to win at the end of the tether
With the still nestling wages in the best of our kola trades and markets!
In quest of a moneyed kola nut, cowries and *marks* one markets far off
To elope in all weathers by turns anew with a rare work of art together,
And renew to stir up what at best snubs lies but far tills grains of truth!
Every truth endures for good like a fresh lily of the sacred peace plants
To awake banners of peace, friendship and unity we nurse in kola nuts!
So, we grade all with ritual cupfuls of wines to wake silent oblivion up
And revive relics of art works we never willingly send on pilgrimage!

10

Oft, graced with palm wine,
A pure kola nut for an ancestor,
Ritually marks a tattoo of its taboo
Within the bulwarks of its open arms,
To set flu virus or grain of justice at war!
A taboo on the first kola fruits and palm-wine
From the farmlands we still till with naked hands,
Severs us out of rustic time to implant in an ecstasy,
As we plant and crop kola trees, nurse and tap palm trees,
Wiser prying eyes offer the spirit world to consume at will,
And duly bless kola fruits and palm wine of age with a choice
To grow up cures in hills, plains and valleys, ancestral spirits set
As an escape route from a self-delusion to defile repentance at will,
Once we forgive to forget the unforgivable in dialogues of kola nuts!

A kola tree in life grows from birth to death,
As part of a kola seed God creates and hallows,
Within a kola pod with the unerring hands of grace,
Ever nestling it between the props and ladders of age!
Once sown, a kola seed may soon sprout up fully *in vivo*,
Even when an *in vitro* world of mixed blessings eclipses it!
Driven as if in a taxi one boards and pays to freely share seats
At various costs with wayfarers duly saddling within a life-span,
We take our share of kola lobes together with attendant taxi drivers,
Who backward and forward neither speed up nor slow down, but go!

Like our trade in beads, cowries and salt,
We plant kola to crop and eat, sell and buy!
Kola makes the pulse of family ties to quicken
Worldwide with gains and interest rates over sea
And desert shores rather than salaries and bonuses!
A kola liturgy blesses a yield with ritual cattle, fowls,
Fruits and tubers we yearly crop from games and names
We update with idiomatic eponyms of heroes and heroines
In fields where an oracular astrologer feeds kola pods at will!
So, kola fruits grease the wheels of kola gifts, snacks and trades,
But ritually, every incoming season heralds tasty foods and drinks,
Under the sway of hospitality as under the influence of its kola rites!
We offer a handshake of thanksgiving to spice new embers of hopes!

A ritual of kola fruits unfurls a flag
Of unseen horizons beyond the handshakes
We oil to share in ingredients of a kola meal!
A kola kernel of truth sprouts up on the ground,
Where wayfarers of age tame but untold kola games,
To rally compatriots under a new banner of patriotism,
Free from the kola politics with notes to divide and rule!
Free too from the kola intrigues of every deceit and malice!
Free from the wiles over the silent currencies of utter bribery,
A new leadership mixes in daily consensus of unsparing norms!
Oft, together as oil in the water of bribery and corruption the kola
God, leaders and people mutually hire blazes a trail in a consensus!
A kola nut we share to chew over in a free dialogue never fully ends!

11

Among rivals, kola nuts win
At best through a martyr's crown!
Today, kola fruits solely take refuge
In the persistent toll of monsoon winds!
A master's machine cuts down kola forests
Within the world of high-tech like a river breaks
Ways noisily down rocky banks with a metal glow
That eclipses kola fruits with *its tender master's voice*!

Today, the kola trade suffers
Also from the *ntèm-ntém* influenza
As it ever does from the parasitic plants
And metal to feed on an upright kola tree!
Blown by winds, a kola tree drops ripe pods
And sheds its dry branches and leaves together,
To regain enough of its nutritious self-same diet!

Like pigs, kola forests swim in the mud,
As today kola fruits sink into the sandy rivers
With poor *kaáyá* prices, wrestling with rivals in a world
Where sheer bribery still usurps the thrones of kola names!
A huge goat arrives from your village as your small kola nut!
Clever or not, a student *envelopes* sums in search of a free entry
Into State Schools on a '*man know man*' basis as a small kola nut!
One by one, brave pioneers abandon just courses for tiny kola nuts!
Corrupt people in uniform connive with thieves for a better kola nut!
Often, a public duty turns into a tacit private fee as a small kola nut!

Mindless of a morrow, the philosophy
Of *lìm bvà' é wùn* seeks but a bodily pleasure
In the kola nut a patient toils to break and chew!
A philosophy of *yàr a yìì ka* invites a small kola nut
From an idler as a fee for odd jobs rather than idleness!
A philosophy of *chop-me-a-chop* exchanges bribes at will,
Backbiting and lobbying rather less in terms of public gains!
A philosophy of *a-goat-eats-where-it-is-tethered* keeps the rift
Between the rich and the poor, as it promotes egoism at its best!
A philosophy of *all mea maxima culpa*, timely calls for a rebirth!

12

A kola nut rotates
From palm to palm in truth
Free from deceit, but within its days
And nights in zones even where kola trees
Survive in songs as between hope and despair!
Yearly, we crop ritual dances and turn a blind eye
To bribery in our luxurious homes of alien hospitality!
We do trade kola in body and mind to draw a soulful gaze
At sheer luxury and poverty, seeking the water level of baits!
Free from bribery and corruption, a kola nut opens up free roads,
Despite liturgies of songs, intrigues and games from birth to death!
Set in bribery and corruption, a kola lobe tears a patriotic flag apart!

The hungry totter better
With a huge kola nut in sight!
Every exchange of handshakes goes
Beyond the threshold of one's childhood
As abruptly as beyond one's old doors of age,
Whither children on the spot may no longer offer
The first hand-picked kola pod with pride to parents
And visitors alike as a spontaneous act of hospitality!

In an offer
Of a kola nut,
One never takes
A no for an answer!
One thanks to the fullest
Without a definite thank-you!
So one neither denies nor accepts,
An offer of every kola nut definitely!
Politeness excels in an offer of kola nuts!
No one offers a kola nut never to offer again!
We offer a kola nut to still offer again and again!
A kola nut to share commands its own airs of graces!
We count our blessings with the kola lobes we share!

13

A lion may stalk its prey
And stroll from field to field,
Or a fugitive may stalk the streets
As birds may stroll into the heavens,
Or ants and worms emerging from soils
May infest crops, trees and weeds together!
Kola trees emerge from the soil heavenwards
With roots firm in the ground and with branches
Praying to prophesy with the praying mantis until
A kola pod buds and matures for a healthy harvest!

A forest of kola trees
As a basket of kola nuts
In every kola market, grows
With the stories of older markets
Where pockets of slaves took a rest
With head-loads of kola seeds to plant
In memoriam of the lost but remembered,
Heroic slaves who died in transit *pro patria*,
Though as neophytes, nursed to trade in kola!

A donkey's cartload outweighs
A head-load of kola seeds in a *kaáyá*!
Bàá Mbaàéwiì, notorious for head-loads,
Enriching and earmarking him with nicknames,
A rare carrier of one thousand two hundred kola seeds,
Trekking for months from home to a far-off kola market,
Where, still instead of cars and planes, over the steps of Sóv,
And *Ntáaba* along the *Sábóngàrí* valley, up the slopes of *Lä Kòv*
Across fences of *Màyò Kaárí* to *Gèmbú* we foot over plains to *Yoolà*,
Whither a song turns a weighty *kaáyá* lighter from *Ngóloojì* to *Yoolà*!
Ee kaáyá wor aa, A m sí lavlàvìn! Á mo mò-oò kó' bam ji! A m sí laàv!
With head-loads, I'm worn out at every step! So uphill, I went in song!
Today, a trader travels in cars, lorries, planes and ships as a bird builds
A nest with plastic papers and old cloth on eaves in a lush kola shrine!
Nature evenly shares dividends of wisdom to all wayfarers on its deck!

Today, lorries or planes race
Still with our kola *kaáyá* parcels
As we also trickle head-loads on steps
Down deep cliffs at sunset and wrestle up
The slopes from mountainous *Màŋgàn Peétèn*,
To *Màŋgàn* and *Gèmbú* at sunrise, mirroring smiles
Of kola trees, grown in memoriam of victims and victors!
There, a suitor's dreams hasten our steps for richer kola sells
And an eager return home to tender the growth of a kola *Fondom*
Where we take and give a daughter's hand through rituals of wedlock!

We weave baskets
Of kola seeds into a forest
With every thread of hospitality
And the diplomacy of luxuriant politics
In kola trades and music of the knowledge,
We religiously till with songs of a plural ritual!
As of old, *ŋgòn juù* oils odd kola trees with camwood,
For *elders* to ritually off-root with palm-wine and awaken,
Folks and crops together within unending traditions of peace!

Our children discover
The thirst of every kola nut
Within the taste of its own lobes,
As with the excitement of a neophyte!
But experts label the name of a kola tree,
By dint of a kola age, popularity and species!
Some kola lobes rival milk, coffee, tea and beer
In taste, but once a tasty kola nut betroths palm-wine,
Or whole kola nuts season thirsty mouths with groundnuts,
We drive idleness with apt kola games, proverbs and riddles,
As we rejoice over a newborn and ritualize those born into death!

IV

Open Kola Nut Baskets

An Open Kola Nut Basket

A kola nut to split and share opens a lively *makarapaati* anew!
Since teenagers and mad people only like to mimic, a partaker
Keenly celebrates such a kola festival in the open and brings
Both fiends and friends together! Bribery always corrupts,
And shamelessly plays a tricky card with airs and graces,
As it gropes about like a straying toad in broad daylight!
The bribery one nowadays nicknames *kola* or *ŋgòmbò*,
Big or small, still exchanges hands at will, throbbing
And whispering behind sealed doors of both silence
And vows over the sovereignty of its trade pattern,
Many readily baptize as *l'ennemi dans la maison*,
Or confusedly easily take for a mixed blessing!
Bribe experts play hide-and-seek like mice -
Longstanding parasites and unchain guests,
Though in residence, ever as destructive
As an intolerable leakage in the roof
Of every home without watchdogs
And vigilant cats ready to wildly pounce
On such a spiteful madness beyond justice!

Patterns of Open Kola Nut Baskets

"…Good men (and women) will not consent to govern for cash or honours. They do not want to be called mercenary for exacting a cash payment for work of government, or thieves for making money on the side; and they will not work for honours, for they aren't ambitious."
Plato: *The Republic*, 347b. Translated by Desmond Lee (1981) Penguin

" 'Pleading' was a regular occurrence in the Limba village life. … If a husband has acted badly, the wife goes to her parents; the husband comes there for her and pleads for the wife to agree to return. The husband gives kola to the wife's people. Then they go and question her about what it was that made her go away, about what the husband is pleading. Sometimes the husband asks the wife's younger sister to plead for him with their mother. The sister goes to the mother, saying that the husband has confessed to doing evil, he is pleading. The husband must wait humbly. Even if they curse him and say bad words, he must not reply, he is ashamed, he can say nothing. Sometimes he goes to an old man and gives him kola and pleads, saying that he will not (act wrongly) again. So the old man goes to help the husband to plead with the wife's family. However much they say against him the husband must not reply. The old man may go in private into the room with the wife, and give her wine, and speak well with her to make her agree to return…"
Ruth Finnegan: *The Oral And Beyond – Doing Things with Words in Africa*. pgs. 33-34. 2007, James Curry Oxford, The University of Chicago Press, The University of KwaZulu-Natal Press

"On the morning after the village crier's appeal the men of Umuofia met in the market-place and decided to collect without delay two hundred and fifty bags of cowries to appease the white man. They did not know that fifty bags would go to the court messengers, who had increased the fine for that purpose."
Chinua Achebe: *Things Fall Apart*. p. 177, 1972 (1958) Heinemann

14

An ad-lib offer of a kola pod by design here now invites
Kola baskets to stand upright in the heyday of fights!
Be it at home or abroad, watchful birds of a feather
In droves as alone augur kola sales in all weather!
One decks kola baskets full to the brim as a gift,
Or rare fodder for dry beaks to prick bit by bit
And thrive in a farm we till and sow to crop
Open yields from a kola seedling we prop!
Sooner or later peace offerings exchange
A flaming row over what they change!

Free from the hands of thieves, we crop a plentiful supply
Of kola fruits to eat, sell and downrightly use to apply
Brakes to ruin bribery and theft! A kola harvest drills
The youth in the art of stealing kola pods, not bills!
Yet, each good deed deservedly steals our thunder
Of a Fon's greetings* for our symbol of thanks!
God takes us aback to drive apt youth asunder,
And sacredly steals to reform our main planks!
On ways to Jericho, on crosses at Calvary,
Thieves lead parasitic lives as primary!

Angels, devils and humans survive in the world
In the sole hands of fair *Nyùy Mbóm* chiseling
As ever sustaining all worldly minds together!
A human devil bribes at the end of my tether
To corrupt freely! Bribery is ever whistling
Its illegal kola deals within a healthy fold!
Mens Sana, in corpore sano, keeps a hold
On its firm truth for centuries and miles,
But bribery secretly derails and defiles
What ushers peace into our world!

We offer a kola basket to open doors of hospitality,
As we plant kola forests to uphold our patriotism!
Mutual hospitality buds in an upright patriotism,
At best, arm in arm as birds of a feather at play!
At worst, as bedfellow in a scramble to display
Far-off sea shores and next-door desert-shores,
Where fish and camel daily search in and out ·
For an era of twin patriotism and hospitality
To bespeak a kola patriotism from without
As from within ocean and desert-shores!

A new patriotism sprints to catch a kola trade for notes
As it creates to overpower poverty rather by the gun
Than by the humane dividend one tills as footnotes
Like coffee, rubber or tea to crop in the short run
For the world market where all are out and out
To dupe and downrightly take a turn to tout
In gain as in rule when the chips are down
And kola pods beneath kola trees crown
An adult or child's day with kola nuts
And tasty sweets *made in....* for sale
Like a big handful of groundnuts,
With which to chew kola or kale!

A change in the drumming changes a dancing-step!
Once a cockerel of age flaps its wings, it crows!
A new musical play of *Haaleluuya* maps a step
To draw attention for a dance-song that grows
For sharp ear-catchers to fully dance at once,
Where a drummer's voice merits a kola nut
With the plural or superlative dance-hunts,
That steals the hands of a *Fon* off the nut
And praises *Nyùy Mbóm* with the voices
Of all fathers and mothers and children
Rather than have an angel to rejoice
Over a live-dance in a split-second!

Quite often at moments you least expect,
You luckily pick one or more kola pods,
To offer an alien as a friend you detect!
Rich power corrupts a ruler on the nod
As kindness turns poor rulers stronger
At heart, but thirstily full of hunger!
A kola gift crowns as it blesses all
Rich and poor with its ever small
But great wars against bribery
And corruption in the name
Of a genuine kola forgery
That battles with fame
To win and deserve
A cup of victory
To fairly serve
A kola story
Of palm wine,
While we dine!

Rather than reign, acts of stealing deprive
Owners of their due shares of kola nuts!
At times tricks of reason even drive
Sheer bravery to roll like coconuts
A thief, in agony as in need, loves
To steal and rear as exotic doves!
The upright fully hates to steal,
As secretly as the house mice
Whose total refusal in a deal
Of theft knows no sacrifice,
To free them from theft!

15

A kola trader deals with all kinds of thieves:
Some friends, some aliens, others relatives!
Unlike a witch, a thief knows no bounds!
As an early leg of theft begins at home,
The last in handcuffs out of bounds,
Though for some, not as a doom,
But as a misfortune to lock up
Like an HIV door or box
Already keyed up!

We plant every kola tree of justice in freedom
At the centre of human life in spite of weeds
A redeeming saviour crops from Golgotha,
At the navel embryo of a sinful universe,
Where all saints grow as they harvest
Crops that cure rather than weeds,
Fraught with perils of ruins,
Between birth and death
In sanctity!

More out of persuasion than coercion,
We plant, harvest and eat kola nuts,
In peace as in wars of liberation!
From a zero to a plus one-year,
We struggle with ground-nuts
For fear to drop more a tear
Of defeat than of victory
And its open story!

Oft, a pure kola nut exchanges few hands,
Out of a mutual pride to promote bribes
With arrogance and deprive set tribes
Of proven humility to offer kola nuts
As sheer kindness in humane lands!
With a difference in fair equality,
One skillfully shares kola nuts,
As an umbrella of the reality,
One errs to cover alone!

One breaks a choice kola nut and shares,
To speak as if in tongues of rarer wares
With kola traders as vigilant in a place
As hunting within their days of grace
To pet tiny villages of a world-trade,
And earn living wages of the bread,
They bake out of a partial equality,
The wise oft grade in self-defence,
As an integral identity of reality,
Breathing within its difference!

As a new Cameroon-Nigerian peace-plant of change
In Bakasi, from East to West, from North to South,
A Barack Obama bravely gives birth to the hopes
We share in the rainbow as kola nut face to face,
Awaiting the sunrise of what feeds the mouth
And mind through an *eco-ethical* exchange
We tether in an open vigil with kola ropes
Within a step life refreshes in the race!

Unlike dreams, kola trees assure a morrow's fruit of inference,
While a kola theft ever deprives everyone of our ownership,
Though more in space than in time's spoken references!
For, fast or slow, ambitions grow with the worship
And tillage of our kola trades in space and time!
A mother hen warms her chickens with wings,
But we nestle under a kolaly world that flings
The swords of rivalry to inflame our times!

Here, as the full cups rally the lucky hands around a mouth,
A basket of kola notes play at a seesaw of lullaby rhymes,
In freedom and in peace to blossom both north and south
Of a people's own hopes and despair in turbulent times!
A kola nut one oft shares to speak in a *Heimatssprache,*
Will referee the monotony of tautology in a movement
To measure the bi-crime beyond measure *zur Sache*!
Freedom fighters truly christen every embezzlement
One fully baptizes with a first name of *A Kola Nut,*
And a last name of *a bribe* to gain a worthy bride!
Once, its leafy birthmarks turn yellow to dry off,
A kola tree gives the needs in due time to cry of
As life shelters and wakes one up free to ride
Over a yawn one stifles as a bit of a yawn
To tackle obstacles to peace at the dawn
Of great ambitions silent in a kola nut!

16

With riddles of its proverbs as stories of its histories,
A kola nut as our world in miniature at best seasons
Every state in the making with proverbial riddles!
A litmus test of a kola lobe sets a conference call
On values of friendship and a factory of reasons
That moves mountains and renews credit titles!
A kola nut we eat, oft tells but our by-stories,
How we fall to rise up but never fail to win!
Kola nuts speak in a number as a safety pin!
Bòŋàtàn, in praise of five as a kola lobe spins!
Bòŋàbaà, in praise of two as kola twins!
Bòŋàdzòm, in praise of all, for all in all!

A kola nut energizes us to endear a giver to a receiver!
A kola nut cheers one to eat and speak of something!
A kola nut empowers one neither to assert nothing,
Nor take sides too soon about an issue of power!
The kola nut one offers, counts for the blessing
To nurse the poor and the rich, old and young!
Like a zero, kola nuts empower by stressing
To the old and young West, its own power
To beget all and silently subsist all along,
As a master key of gifts open to an offer!
A kola nut tags nothing else but itself!
A kola nut frees all, except itself!

A kind heart willingly crowns a hero with a kola nut!
A kola nut minus a kola nut gives more than a zero!
Often, a kola nut also enkindles old flames that set
A solid house on fire without trading in for a hut!
At times, foes and friends gladly scramble to bet
And offer kola as a widow's mite to their hero,
Who rewards every unity with its difference!
A full kola nut reigns along its numbers,
As inside its plural figure of partakers!
A kola nut, as a matter of reverence
For nothing else but itself, fills
The bill as a plus in its pills!

A kola fruit invites each lover to keep the best company
At heart as a beloved sets out walking on a stony road
Of feats and defeats to win by dint of a timely effort
And foot the bill of a plus figure rather than a zero!
Sharing kola lobes at heart, a lover and a beloved
Together, hand in hand, echo our human family,
Where a junior pleads for a new story's taproot
As elders bless, choose and place a kola peel,
Pod and nut to foretell our world's fortune-
Body, heart and soul at the heart of fruits!

As tiny as it looks, every kola nut reigns
With its crown at the heart of all fruits!
The size or taste of a kola nut feigns
In its smallness or in its bitterness,
But never as a nut of royal fruits!
A kola nut sweetens bitterness
Like a ruler settles eagerness
To succeed more in the arts
Of net justice and fairness,
Than wholly at the mart!

We daily break, share and eat a kola nut of choice,
As casually as ceremonially for the life it gives,
Like the money we need to spend and rejoice,
Or the water we use and drink for the lives,
We nurse along banana bunches at rivalry
To sprout in a place and season as crops!
A worm throbs within a healthy fruit,
As corruption daily spreads in drops
Whispering in every art of forgery,
One at home or abroad still bruits!
Corruption thrives on people,
Ordinary or born in purple!

A law neither ranks persons only by blood nor takes
A kola nut of bribery as corruption for the answer!
A foolish cock fails to crow but the sun still rises
With her splendours to endow whoever partakes
In her indiscriminate sunshine with an adviser!
A kola nut cures wrangling, but fights rivalry!
A kola nut either fuels or quells *kùŋkùsá* talk,
Oft, to redress backbiting, revenge and lying
In a world throbbing far with cruel bribery!
Let bribery ferment to set lies into crisis!

A basket of kola nuts puts everything together
In the world of taste and smell, love and hate!
All that falls apart joins hands again to rise!
We're born to live in the world and gather
Within our times rather than hibernate!
Nothing stands and sits from sunrise
To sunset as the world of daily life!
A mad strife between ripe bribery
And its rumours ends up as rife
With our wars over misery!

Epilogue

From the Kola Gorges where the Shaari meanders,
Between Bakasi and Bomba as between the Cross River
And the Mongo with a memorial kola tree of peace and unity,
Kola forests grow and nestle our joys and sorrows to flow as free
As the rainbow with its colours replete with all gifts of the life-giver!

Of old, Kìmè, Mbàm, Ncaàri Yéèŋ, and Ŋgòn Nso' in free ventures
As in net raptures did sow the kola trees we harvest today to grow
From Ŋkàr and Kitiíwúm over Màyò Kaárí to Gèmbú and Yoolà!
With a kola riddle and a song to turn kaáyá as light as lectures,
We foot on seasons in, season out, at every kolaly cock-crow
With the market *Goorò* to return with *dàvàdává* or a *buútà*,
As ventures and raptures of lectures to trade up the young,
We daily enrich with ripe beliefs, cultures and tongues!

A Change of Heart

A change at heart
Takes place at best
Within the kernel too,
Where a crook turns tail
To become an expert cook -
A cook of all the body feeds on!
A cook of all, the entire mind chews
And digests still to awake at every risk!
A cook of all the life-styles we live in bunches!

Such a baptism changes aspects of life!
A thief pleads aloud for the Lord to pardon
And take a soul into the eternity of the righteous,
Where our earthly sovereigns seek in vain to enter
Even by the narrow gate to discover why it's still open
But to the beggars, old crooks and every wretched of earth,
Who henceforth feast but on the highest table around the Lord,
Simply because they'd fought relentlessly with the arms of truth!
Nothing succeeds in the long run like a fight with the arms of truth!

Business Politics

Once politics becomes a business,
Our human rights will serve to create
The best basis of our faith, rule and trade
And never vanish from the scene of daily life!
Whoever goes in for business politics, will grope
For a way or waddle still across the roads of despair,
Failure and idleness before the dawn of success breaks in!

But whoever goes in for politics
Tout court does not avoid the politics
Of repetition the history of nature teaches
To the people and their leaders in hard times!
The people change leaders rather than the contrary!
Business politics at best heralds the good of the people,
Wherever fairness rather than failure reigns on to succeed!

6th December 2007
Yawunde, Cameroon

Lessons of Tears
(In Memory of Dr. Ignatius Kinyuy +1986)

Kinyuy! God knows why we now bid you farewell! You came unasked!
You've been called home unasked! We've to bid you farewell in tears!
But the pains of our tears no more nurse fears! You're already at home!
Yet, each second drops a tear on the unsalted waters we drank together
in friendship from the calabash that now survives but in broken bits
of fading memories we gather over the red soil of your home!

God knows why we bid you farewell at the dawn of your sunshine!
Farewell then, as a new caravan member of the timeless!
You, a docile child that knew no bounds to errands! In dismay
We sigh out our prayers and clap our hands to eschew the memory
Of our remnant days together as we stood firm on the grounds
Of principles of common fears and common hopes! Kinyuy farewell!
We'll share the oil-and-salt free corn-and bean meal in your memory!

Kinyuy! God knows why you opened new doors of friendship
within the frames of the undying earth we now water with tears
as some now knit their songs of jealousies over trivialities!
Pilgrims! We never came to stay on and on with the clock
Of eternity tick-tocking for the student to become a colleague,
A landsman to become a patron parent among the innocent!
With our heals we revive the drum-beats of our joys and sorrows,
though unable to withhold birth from death in the prime of youth!

God alone knows how to beget life within the egg of life!
But where thrives the exception, if to begin is never to end!
We name a child, *Gò'la* to remind us of our mortality!
The groping child as the centenarian, the upright or the cripple,
a Saint or a criminal, all come to go! Kinyuy! Farewell! *Sii Go˜la!*

2nd February 1986
Paris, France

Relics and Reins

Some we cap with the honesty of the just
And by degrees they reveal themselves,
Cap in hand as initiators and leaders,
Stretching out the lengthening arms of new laws,
Day after day, in accordance with our expectations!

So, we cap new stories of their own making,
And as each accepts a headwear, we earn
A foot-wear of the moderns who walk around
Bare-headed but hardly bare-footed! There,
Generations of post-colonialists pace on, torn
Between slogans of a *chop-me-I-chop*
And a *let-every-goat-eat-around-its-tether's-post*!

Yet, the ancestors pour their graces
On those recalling to recycle ruins of songs
We lost in idioms that sprout the splendour of prosperity!
In ancestral names surviving intact to breathe forth
In our names as in memories of ruins we crop
To replant in and with new testaments of relics
And reins one yodels over hills and plains
As if to telephone more generations to and fro
With the new arts of our age
That now unearth and soothe enriching memories
Of hope rather than despair!

1986
Paris, France

Mistakes

I write to right faults
Long committed within the blindness
Of their times and places
As colonialism deepened its double edge
Of blessings and wounds!

At meals we pray in the foreign name of God
As we greet friends next door in a foreign tongue,
And when we part we greet with a foreign wave
Of the hand and smile a foreign smile – so,
Our charity thus begins abroad, though we're at home
Everywhere away from home!

I write to speak out
About the uncorrected faults
We inherited from the mistakes of parents,
Who believed all was only for a while,
But, everything went on and on beyond bounds
In the clothes we wear as in the food we eat!

Rethinking a mistake, one only errs
If one believes in its rightness again!
I write to right the faults long forgotten
Wherever it began to rain and pour,
For one to realize the umbrella
Of our making had long been kept at home,
Once we were away from home to stay
At home as always at heart!

1983
Bambili, Cameroon

Etudi

Oh Poem,
Emerging within the shadow of my words!
Behold a panegyric I address to your epiphany!
Like palm-wine, I tap you from this Etudi-park
To feed members of the *Njàŋgí*, poets *cook* and share
Dividends between themselves, readers and listeners!
I lure them all out into the open markets of today
Steaming with knowledge and faith as with a dance step,
And a voice within the wilderness of power!

Poem! Fruit of our fruit-trees, I grace thee with a kìkéŋ leaf!
We sing thy praises no more in alien tongues! We tell thy beads
With the lips of this god-fearing Moslem who stands and sits
In rituals of cleansing from head to toe facing the rising sun,
With his water-buútà and mat we baptize *taàburúmá*!

I pamper thee with lullabies
To escape accidents within the city's rhythms!
I'm already leaving Etudi for the better rather than the worse!
I turn my back to you, Yawunde, like soldiers turn their backs
To every battlefield of unattended interests, though resolute
To free thee like a remnant of death on my way to doom,
Otherwise thou be lost in oblivion!

Oh Poem, should thou emerge
From my pen and ink with the evidence of thy birth
Within a second, a day, a year or even a century to come,
Please dismiss the publicity of an endless procrastination
Now lingering at the very fringes of my forested hopes!
We never undo a fair administration in the name of justice!
Now, we're on the brink of crossing the rubicon
In the name of our best prayers against injustice and freedom!

18th February 1989
Bambili, Cameroon

A Teacher's Dream

A poet can admire and marry
flowers with laughter at dawn,
or with tears at noon
but we sing and drum in laughter as in tears!

Let the poet sing
with the voice of prophecy,
with the pen of condemnation,
with a brush of relief,
with the chisel of repairs,
we'll still build with the chorus
of blessings, dreams and hopes!

Let the poet grope on and on
along the thorny highway of ordeals,
we'll lag behind the trail of success
with the lanterns of poetic faith
backwards and forwards!

No poet gropes aimlessly!
A poet lulls children
with a teacher's dream
that listens but looks ahead!
A teacher's voice never fades,
even when his pen or chisel drops!
Like a builder, a teacher builds for the morrow!

4th November 1990
Bambili, Cameroon

On the Laps of Hills*
(In Memory of Bernard Nso'kìka Fònlòn,
Shuúfáay Wóo Ntoòndzàv: 1924-1986.)

Stunned at this port, words escape my mouth
and leave me moonstruck to plough through
such a filial attraction for a mother –
whom we only recently saw off –
causing tides of tears I can no longer control.
Like mother, like son on the laps of the Táayav Hills,
baby-sitters at home with the Fon's eyes and ears and arms
ageing under church-bells: Christian samples on ancestral lands!

A strange journey indeed!
Beguiled with the pleasant talk of the uncapped:
to have flown out intact, prolific, feathered
and with your staff in hand, still feeding on
the corn and the bean, the carrot and the yam,
clothed in the tatters of our own experiences, well shod.
A noble with royal chambers; all told, more reasons for more caps!
So you left in the heyday of our child's glory…
But soon flew back in bits of wood!

A wholesome heart now wrenched off its hinges,
covered with frigid frames, retelling and puzzling
over our cluster of memories of the Lake Nyos, Fumbot…
A handy calabash with which we fetch water from the Kinsaan
to cook and feed all from the Fon to the wretched in the land!
The spittle I swallow rather than add to the waters of my tears,
in prayers will crown you all to shine among the blessed of God!
Your seeds will ever sprout!

A letter-box with writing-utensils, should the telephone fail us
in this world of classical songs issuing from the wireless and the books
we still write with Abbia Stones, recalling the name-giver
and that diviner of the anthem we still consult with grace
to invent and baptize even beyond the Camlines!
A professorial mind curtailed. Nay!
Deprived even of a missionary box!
An inspiring spirit imbued with a sense of creativity,
creeping pumpkinwise; but now within the joinery of foreign nails!

What a twin friendship!
If only our ears can stick to this hearsay...
Should this whispering be repeated in the open?
You'll survive in richer verses!
A handshake I offer still like a shrewd bird perching to take off,
to migrate, before the branch tilts, rehearsing lullabies from brooks
and beyond against the laissez-faire of the age's youth
as they hop, skip and jump on the branches of future centuries,
queuing up behind the pathfinder to renew our initial ceremony
of meals of unsalted corn-and-bean, still as barefooted as bareheaded
with the bare boards of xylophone feats to re-echo the final bridges
you built between nations in the name of friendship as you went home!
At home is best by the Divine! Sojourns on earth only perch! *A ber ne*!

Sunday, 31ˢᵗ August 1986
Southampton, United Kingdom

The Hidden Truth

The winter clouds bore me on from the heavens
fresh with the dignity of a visitor rather than a tourist,
and they welcomed me from the curtains
of their windows with smiles of greetings
which convinced me of having discovered
my lost home within their walls. And I stopped
and slept but dreamt about home
everyday of our eight-day week counting
nothing but their litanies of exorbitant prices
and wayward traps for gain and domination
in commerce, government and even football
though I knew I was a cultural loser
with no other choice but to stick to my mistakes
in the hope that one day they'll change their timetable
and with the lessons from their past
I might live a corrected life of winners
away from the carpets of their stolen wealth.

Thus I ploughed through winter and summer
counting weeks of seven days
and zig-zagging through the irregular months
of their year, eating their salad! And
during those salad days, it now occurs to me
I lived a life of a salamander with no *salama alaikum*
from home to where I patriotically sent letters
to say air and water and body were still in harmony
but wanted to know more about the evils of other days
feasting on bribery and corruption and embezzlement
but nursing nations under the banners of both hospitality
and patriotism in the heart of ruthless tribalism blinding
the growth of endogenous creativity that discriminates none!
We'll nurse the patriotism of our world within hospitality!

17th June 1986
Paris, France

Cameroon: Who Wins?

1.

Soon,
the morrow's stories will open their tales
and what comes alive to us today
from the local stores of the power festivals,
we now attend daily in prayers,
shall even bridge and puzzle the tricky silence
of current and early stories!

For,
beyond the budding daggers in market-places,
and cities we so baptized as the anthills
of our activities and lore today - *proverbially,
once a capital city breathes no more...* the rest
of the country no longer sprawls out or breathes
alert or alive, but turns aflame with famishing tongues
that only lick and seek upright roofs, withered crops
and hand-sewn clothing of every marketable size -
our world has suddenly turned off and fallen into chaos!

Here,
we also witness a crumbling capital city
that turns her troops in disarray
to feed our citizens with desperation
and convert simpletons into schools of thought,
while our old Germanic bastion easily floats along
to give its flames free movement in all directions!

Again I witness folks screaming to get out
of the whirlpools a ghost town made
with banners as if to follow still in the footsteps
of *Anlu'* to bequeath remnants of the day
to *Ta'kembey* while others crop a morrow's game
of injustice at the anthills of a domestic school
biased against fair-minded thinking and acting together!

There, silence issued from the unspeakable!
Patriotism exchanged hands with its horrendous apostasy
sans objet, plein d'actions, but not sans amour de la patrie!
We still speak and write *pour la patrie*, as if in dreams!
Our obsessions of the times were spinning to blossom

the interest we take in stifling hopes, especially
in an era of a definite will to power and enslavement!
For, whoever asked for liberation, was shown
but a wider road into enslavement!

2.

Cameroon!
In dreams, at work and at leisure
we twist you up and down,
backwards and forwards, sideways or round and round
within the vast devouring jaws of the unknown
as within the immense fragile fingers of age,
leaving nothing unsaid nor a stone unturned,
in an attempt to recover our priceless freedom from chains!

Cameroon!
Except with a will to stir and enrich our post-discoveries,
can we still be caught in sacrilegious acts,
stealing as strangers from the altars of our ancestors,
whose bones breathe within your soils,
whose bones you shelter within your gardens,
whose breath you incense in folds
with countless heavenly wreaths of vapour rising
from your seas, lakes and rivers to incense all our offerings!

Cameroon! A *Mànjòŋ* name daily re-baptizes our youth
into Cameroonians of every hue within the rainbow!
We abide by your ways, even within the riots of the day,
provided you are truly ours!
Cameroonians before birth as within our breath!
Cameroonians to desist once you revert
to anything else, but to type!

Cameroon!
We've seen you mirroring our days!
Our dazzling, restless Lions at the Olympics!
Yet, you nurse the burning flames of blood and a hailstorm
of curses from within where we now search but in shame
for worthy standards of excellence! At odds with our days,
we still yearn for the heyday of the old
like a thirsty camel for water, pulsating within
to quicken our pace into the unknown as we yell prayers

in fright for a short-live-Cameroon in blood and flames,
if she be ours! We churn the waves
of soured tears, hopes and fears in confusion,
confession and deceptive corruption
to stress and strain within a new wedlock
of hegemony and illegitimacy!

Cameroon!
Shouldn't thou be still ours, though defaced by woes
for your ripe and unripe fruits of nature's gifts?
How can one differentiate a *waka waka* lady
from a prowling lion who no longer roves
within the tethering dens of our grasslands?
By rambling and rocking to the rhythms of its making,
the sun still pursues its course in the horizon!
But we've become your orphans without a sense of direction!

3.

Today, the sun shines with a person per person vote!
Yet we wallow like pigs in the bloody mire and mess
in our abattoir of forlorn hopes! Everywhere
we live with the tears and flames of a freedom fighter
as we baptize our liberty squares with names
like those of the six maiden victims at Ntarikun,
or with the same influenza that engulfed the Ndu martyrs
amidst constant police plagues that devoured a Ngwa
as its final, serial victim!

Today, the Mungo-Bomba-Shaari triangle excludes
l'ennemi dans la maison in silence
as we breathe but filthy air everywhere!
The filth of devaluations with their sister kin
of bribery and corruption, squandering
and embezzlement of public funds, poisons poverty!
The filth of holy privatization, calumny
and the prostitution of power, promotes hegemony!
The filth of the injustice *par arrangement*
with the guilty, if not favouritism in courts, says it all!
The filth of partisan loyalties now polluting
the consciences and policies of good intentions betrays
more than it does portray!

Today, within the Mungo-Bomba-Shaari triangle we breathe
but the air of criminals without crimes, styled liars and cheats!
The stubborn air of blacklegs and blackmailers pollutes!
The unspeakable air of law officers delaying justice
to inflict but the brute force of the jungle, pours over rocks!
The anathema of schools turned into shameless brothels sings!
The filthy air of enflamed K-towns turned hostage by dint of a hunt
for drinking water to quench waterless villages shouts!
The anathema of victims looted and bleeding their last
without the minimum medical care shames everybody!

Today, within the Mungo-Bomba-Shaari triangle
torture keeps us on the trot with its Trojan-horses of power,
withdrawing to reduce salaries at will
and sap justice away from remnants of a colonial knitting!
Torture disarms with the colonial wheels of thinking,
as food, shelter and clothing now enthrone
a market-economy of their own making!
Deforestation whispers its showers of *zero-mort*
where victims once fell to sprout no more
as sweat turned into tears and tears into blood,
where we skip abuses, plagues and woes
to confront funerals on every landscape!
Pillage and piracy rendered everyone a loser
who no longer dares to summon our sold minds
to the task of who wins in these utter flames of misery!

1994
Bambili / Bamenda, Cameroon

65

Our First Aid Boxes

Let the wisdom of Manjoŋ and Takembeŋ assist us
To say our day's say against robbery in broad daylight!
Corruption no longer credits the power of prevention
That miraculously cures more than the best first aid boxes!

Bitter truth always hurts victims, especially
When it directly steps on their weak toes!
One surprises a consumer in an attempt to escape
From the misdeeds of bribery we try to wrap up
With interest behind daily scenes in taxis and offices!

A taxi passenger who shames rather than cheers up
A law-officer with a keen eye or ear of censure,
Already mockingly waters but the garden of justice,
Where corruption never grows even for a while in fame!

Yet, shifty law-officers reconnoitre suitable grounds
For a sizable portion of Ŋgòmbò or palm wine
Behind closed doors with clients like the taxi-drivers,
They bark out orders to update their first aid boxes,
Their taxi-vignettes, in order to bite a marked page
With a five hundred francs or more for a daily njàŋgí!

Law-officers and taxi-drivers begin to *cook but a njàŋgí,*
Once the whistle blows for a stop in intimacy!
Prevention here surpasses a cure,
Though the weevils of corruption gnaw at the heart
Without complete first aid boxes or elixir!
A mayday call like an SOS never sets hands
On our first aid boxes in the right places!
So, the culprits vanish into thin air!

21st October 1996
Yawunde, Cameroon

Glossary of Notes and Explanations

- *Les choses qui arrivent aux autres commencent à m'arriver*! The French for *what happens to others is beginning to happen to me*. We are quoting it from a vcd collection of songs (2005) as a tribute to the reputed Cameroonian musician, Bobe Yerima Afo-Akom, alias Taa Manjong, and his various teams of dancers.

- *Res publica*: The Latin for *a public affair, a public thing, what belongs to the public eyes and ears and by implication what belongs to the state as a people.*

- *Mbií-Fòn*: The Lam Nso' for the Fon's *Mbií*, a durable hard seed of a fruit tree by the same name; Though *Bara'* means a foreigner, here it means the Western European culture.

- *A red feather* is an award in acknowledgement of a great deed!

- *Every bòbí naà wân* is a proverb in *Cameroon Pidgin English*. It means that every breast exhibits the same qualities. To judge from its form of *All bòbí / bòbí naà wân* (*Every breast is one/the same*), it connotes both an identity and a difference at the same time.

- To throw the first stone – recalls the message of Jesus in the Gospel of John, 8: 1-11.

- *Gàlúrí* is a type of colouring powder or bluish paint known by this name in many Cameroonian and Nigerian languages.

- Archaic Tiŋékari term, *Ŋgòŋ* means contextually in English: world, earth, and universe.

- A house of "Ŋwéròŋ or a house of Ŋgírì , could be translated from the Lam Nso' with some losses of, and gains in, dividends, as *A house of commons or a house of Lords*.

- Before the Western colonial era, such localities as *Sov, Támnyàm, Bòkídé', Yoolà and Wèrìmaayò* were and are still today, to a certain extent, kola markets beyond Nso', the seat of kola forests.

- *Kaáyá* is a Hausa language name for a head-load, or luggage as was carried on donkeys or later in cars and lorries. *Kaáyá* usually connotes the transportation of kola seeds, generally known as kola nuts, hence, its meanings of a heavy bundle or a burden.

- *Foofoo* corn, pronounced as *fúfú corn*, is a type of food prepared with corn, unlike *mendóndó*, which is prepared with cassava.

- In Lam Nso' *Nyùy Mbóm* translates the idea of the 'Ever-creating God' as opposed to '*God the Creator*'.

- *Wen tru tori de swit, tif man de laf fo banda!* Pidgin English for *Once a true story is enjoyable, even a thief will laugh from a hide-out* (and betray his presence) *in the ceiling.* Denis Diderot (1713-1784), one of the well-known secularist philosophers of the French Enlightenment, once wrote that 'Alas the beauty of virtue is such that its image is respected even by brigands in the depth of their caverns.' Although the idea here is that even thieves take a share in an enjoyable story to the extent of violating their rule of silence, the meaning is apparently that, between themselves, brigands observe rules of behaviour which are analogous to the laws of society at large.' Cyprian Ekwensi, a Nigerian novelist, in a novel entitled, *Nana Yagua*, makes one of the characters who is a thief to express himself in the following terms to other thieves: "Whatever profession you do, you must do it well," which I quote from memory, without being a partisan of the underlying fallacy. Stealing is a vicious practice that surprisingly follows certain norms.

- *Primus possedentis*: Latin for *the first owner*, or the first person to pick a kola pod and own it in such a way that the person alone can decide what to do with it.

- *Njò'* are the Lam Nso' for the divinatory portions of kola peels, parings, pods or seeds.

- We have often made distinctions between an adjectival and noun uses of kola, kola nut, kola seed, kola pod and kola tree, but there are no corresponding verbal or adverbial forms, such as *to kola or kolaly*. One can still, however, speak of *to kola an occasion* i.e. to provide kola to attendants of an occasion, and of *a kolaly occasion*, i.e. an occasion whereby attendants receive kola nuts from their host or an occasion suitable for serving kola nuts.

- *Ee Yéèŋ wor á, àá Yéèŋ!*: A refrain of a well-known Lam Nso' song that depicts how Ŋgòn Nso' yearned for her missing Ncaàrì Yéèŋ after their historical departure from Rifəm. The rest of the Lam Nso' text in this basket as in the next have their translations immediately after the text.

- *Baàbá (Olée), yaàyà yóò! Maàmá (Olée), yaàyà yóò* is a common affectionate expression of welcome from children to parents.

- '*Oo Gracious God, You see what the whiteman did, hm, hm, hm!*' is an adapted African-American spiritual that covers two of our kola nut baskets here and depicts the horrendous events of the *Transatlantic Slave Trade.* It's one of the *Negro spirituals* that speak for themselves by depicting the collective as well as the anonymously telling picture of the *Transatlantic Slave Trade.*

- *Wann und wo sehen wir uns wieder und sind froh?* German for: 'When and where shall we meet again and be happy?' (Our translation).

- *Mein Hahn ist todd. Er kann nicht mehr singen Krokudil, Krokus dein.* German for: 'My cock is dead! It can no longer sing crocodile, your crocus.' (Our translation).

- Each idea has a tenacity that depicts a rope with which a weaver plaits a basket. As such, short or long sentences that express an idea equally depict a rope of their own tenacity in words.

- *Ŋgòn juù* verbally, 'a maiden or a girl of marriageable age,' but technically women of the owner's lineage who officially exercise the right to cut down or ritually initiate a willful elimination of a kola tree among the Nso'.

- *Bíy Kimbàŋ* verbally, the kola (*bíy*) of the red person (*Kimbàŋ*). Here it means a kola tree which relates to the story of colonial powers in Nso', unlike *Bíy yeé Pànyá* which indicates a Nso' compound whose owner had been to Equatorial Guinea, a former Spanish colonial territory. *Pàenyaà* relates indirectly to Spain and Spanish, but directly to Equitorial Guinea. Some of the Nso' who had been to this part of the world, spoke so much about it that the rest of the Nso' nicknamed their compounds, *Pànyá.*

- *Shaà cér aá wàá lo! Caà ceé aá vaàvàá lo!* Our interest is in the evident phonological differences when an adult and a child speak.

- The *Afo-a-Kom* is a work of art which was returned to Cameroon after it had been stolen away. Its return was such a sensational experience that today it still inspires and connotes any work of art that comes back to its original home after an elopement.

- *Ntèm-ntém* is influenza, a kind of parasite that attacks kola trees.

- *'Lìm bvà' é wùn'* verbally, 'work and consume' in Lam Nso' is a kind of *Epicureanism*, distinct from the philosophy of *'Yàr á yii ka'*, a lack of a better choice that obliges one to accept the first offer of any job, irrespective of one's own choice, and from the philosophy of *a chop-me-a-chop* or 'gains for each interested party', is a kind of bribery and corruption whereby the participants agree to share dividends between themselves.

- Among the Nso', the white and black colours of the *Ŋwéròŋ* staff as well as the blue and white colours of *Ndzày njav* are the nearest image to the colours of a zebra or a zebra crossing.

- *The Fon's greetings:* The Nso' consider it the best and highest symbol of gratitude to clap hands to someone else other than their Fon. Hence the symbolic expression of stealing the Fon's hands to thank somebody who has performed an exceptional deed.

- *Makarapaati:* Etymologically from the Hausa term, *Makaranta* (school) and the English term, party.

- *l'ennemi dans la maison:* French for 'the enemy within the house'.

- *Eco-ethical* is a term inspired by the eco-ethical philosophy of aretology as expounded by the renowned Japanese philosopher, Tomonobu Imamichi.

- *Heimatssprache,* the German for 'home spoken-language'.

- *Sache,* the German for 'thing', but the phrase, *zur Sache* means 'relevantly to the point.'

- *Kùŋkùsá*: is a term like *ashia* (sorry) that has become a common coin in Cameroon languages. It means a kind of backbiting, but in certain contexts it seems to strike a balance between blackmailing and backbiting. *Kùŋkùsá* is a spiteful conversation about someone else mainly in his or her absence. It also means rumour.

- *Gwàgwá* means a duckling in the Hausa language.

- A *should-in-case* is an expression that means a useful and sizeable plastic paper bag or any light bag (Cameroonian) women usually carry along as they travel in case they find or buy something unexpected to bring home.

- *Mànjòŋ* is a collective Tiŋékari name for men's associations or clubs.

- The Kom *Anlu'* and the Ngemba *Ta'kembeŋ* are women's associations with a certain degree of political power.

- *Sii Go˝la* rhetorically means who really remains?

- **Présence Africaine** N0. 139 published the first version of this poem.

- *A ber ne*! in the context is the Lam Nso' for *till we will meet again*.

71